About the author

Chuck Spezzano, Ph.D. is a world-renowned counsellor, trainer, author, lecturer and visionary leader. He holds a Doctorate in Psychology. From 30 years of counselling experience and 26 years of psychological research and seminar leadership, Dr Spezzano and his wife, Lency, created the breakthrough therapeutic healing model Psychology of Vision. The impact of this model has brought deep spiritual, emotional and material change to thousands of participants from around the world.

Also by Chuck Spezzano

If It Hurts, It Isn't Love
Wholeheartedness
50 Ways to Find True Love
50 Ways to Let Go and Be Happy
50 Ways to Change Your Mind and Change the World
    (available March 2002)

50 Ways to Get Along With Absolutely Anyone

CHUCK SPEZZANO, Ph.D.

CORONET BOOKS
Hodder & Stoughton

First published in Great Britain in 2001 by Hodder and Stoughton
A division of Hodder Headline

A Coronet Paperback
10 9 8 7 6 5 4 3 2 1

A CIP catalogue record for this title is available from the British Library.

ISBN 0 340 79353 8

Typeset by Palimpsest Book Production Limited,
Polmont, Stirlingshire
Printed and bound in Great Britain by
Mackays of Chatham plc, Chatham, Kent

Hodder and Stoughton
A division of Hodder Headline
338 Euston Road
London NW1 3BH

This book is dedicated to Karl and Enid Abel.

To my mother-in-law, Enid Abel, for your generosity and for always being on my side. It is said, 'Behind every successful man is a surprised mother-in-law.' You have been a true gift for me, one for whom I've never needed this book.

To my father-in-law, Karl Abel, for your generosity and presence in my life; when my father died, from the depths of your heart you said, 'I will be your father now.' Thank you for that forever.

Weeks before I met them, I heard a voice say to me in a meditative state: 'You are about to be given a great gift. You are to be given another set of parents.' This book is written in appreciation for that great gift. Thank you, Mom. Thank you, Dad.

Acknowledgements

I want to thank Peggy Chang, Kathy Strobel and Jane Corcoran for your long hours of typing. To Jane Corcoran, Heidi Ainsworth, Elizabeth Kewin and Karen Sullivan for making this a better book through your editing and comments; you were invaluable. To Sue Allen, agent extraordinaire, thanks for all the encouragement, help and liaison. Thanks everyone, for your faith and friendship! Also Lucie Mattar, assistant and supporter, who kept everything running smoothly when all of us were just running.

When it comes to a team effort, I want to acknowledge my wife, Lency and my children for all their love, support and inspiration.

Finally I want to acknowledge *A Course in Miracles,* for the central part it has played in my life. Throughout this book, you will find principles that I learned through *A Course in Miracles*. Across the years, I have made many 'discoveries', ideas and principles that I believed had never been previously recorded. Until, of course, I found *A Course in Miracles*. It corroborated what I had found and showed me much more.

Contents

Preface

It seems to me that, given half a chance, we can find someone with whom to have a problem. This can result in distractions, traps, conflict and pain. Any problem with another person is the reflection of a conflict with ourselves. What we hate in others we hate in ourselves, and it is blockages from within that generate invisible walls in our lives that stop us from love, from moving forward and from success.

As happy relationships are the key to the experience of joy in our lives, it seemed important to provide a simple book of principles that, when needed, could be there like an old friend. May this book serve you in good times, as well as when the road seems dark and threatening. There is an old Korean proverb that says, 'Even if the sky should fall, there is a way out.' There always is a way out if you are willing to see things differently. May this book bless you with a way out and the way in, not only to others' hearts and minds, but to your own.

Warmest aloha,

Chuck Spezzano
Hawaii, 2001

Introduction

This book is for both beginners and the advanced. It is meant to grow as you do so that when you come back to it in, say, six months or two years, it will be waiting to take you on your own personal healing journey once more. Some of the concepts are repeated two or three times in this book, sometimes as minor points in a chapter and sometimes later as a whole chapter. Some chapters build on each other and others return to the same theme from different angles, giving more or in-depth information because of the importance of the subject.

Written synchronistically, this book can serve you if you intuitively choose three numbers between 1 to 50 and then study those chapters as they apply to your problem. It may be easier to do this once you have read and worked through the whole book, because some of the concepts are uncommon or subconscious principles. You might mark the three chapters you instinctively chose and read them with particular interest as you get to them. When you finish the book you might guess another three ways to review.

While it isn't necessary to do the exercises, this will make the book transformational rather than simply informational for you. You may find some of the material difficult on first reading, but allow the message to plant a seed in your mind and you'll find that new understanding and self-understanding will grow. A later reading will crystallise any unclear messages.

This book isn't meant to be religious but it is unabashedly spiritual. I have found the spiritual to comprise a natural part of our minds, along with the artistic, the psychic, and shamanic parts. In its final essay, our evolution evolves in a spiritual direction and I have found these spiritual metaphors to work in Asia, Africa, North America and Europe, regardless of religious faith or belief.

The book is set up to work easily if you practise one way every day, but you will find your most effective pace as you travel through.

WAY 1 Those We Dislike are on Our Team

The most important aspect of our lives is our attitude, because our attitude defines the direction in which we are heading. Our attitude is created out of continuous decisions made in a certain direction. Therefore, it is most important that we choose a life that has a giving, regenerating, youthening, and abundant direction. If we do not, our chances of knowing love and happiness are slim.

Life can seem like a war in which we are fighting for our families, while others outside us threaten us and our security. Of course, it's sometimes our families at war. If we choose an attitude of 'us against them', it will subtly (or not so subtly) translate itself into relationship problems with those we love the most. We will not be safe from the competition, power struggle, and fear that we see so blatantly existing in the world around us. It is most important to choose an attitude that will unite us with our partners, our families and the outside world.

The spiritual insight of 'love your enemies' was brought to earth by Christ, but as a psychological means to heal and transform situations it is little recognised and even more rarely practised. We have the opportunity to turn our enemies into our allies, our teammates and even our saviours. This is the highest attitude to take towards those around us. As we truly succeed with one person in our lives, by transforming him or her into an ally, we simultaneously evolve all of our other relationships into being more supportive and healthy.

Those we dislike represent a lesson we are being asked to learn. To learn this lesson advances our maturity, our confidence, our ability to make contact and our ability to receive. To learn the lesson of turning a seeming enemy into an important ally advances our leadership, increases our power and truly helps the world around us.

Throughout my in-depth work in psychology I have seen this demonstrated time and time again, both inside and outside healing sessions and workshops. I have been told many hundreds of times by those who had just been in a workshop and healed themselves in some manner, how they had gone home and found that their mate, child, parent or mother-in-law had changed.

It is possible to change the world around us by changing ourselves. This book is a practical means by which we can do just that. It will give us the tools, but we must provide the willingness and attitude necessary to make the changes. It will require us to 'get off our positions'. Whenever we are stuck we are unable to learn, because at a subconscious level we are hiding a conflict within. We can change all of this through our willingness to be wrong about this situation – because if we are right about it, if it is exactly how we think of it, if the person with whom we are not getting along is precisely how we say they are, then we are stuck with the situation as it is.

If we are willing to learn, willing to be mistaken, then the case is not closed and things can change. We now have a chance of happiness. We are not victims, we are empowered. No matter how vicious, dishonest or evil the person with whom you are not getting along seems to be, the principles contained within the conflict have a primordial power to transform the situation at hand. The key question is, do we have the willingness to learn and change ourselves? If we are not willing to change our experience of the situation, it will remain the same.

One of the biggest mistakes we make in relationships is to act as if the other person has been put on earth to meet our needs, to make us happy and to do things 'our way.' Someone can only upset us if they have not lived up to the script that we assigned to them; we can only be upset if they have not lived their lives according to our expectations. This is a misuse of relationships. It turns people into objects, mere supporting actors and actresses in the play in which we are the star, director and producer. No one can fail or even betray us. They just do not act in the ways we have assigned them to act. They just do not play the parts we have silently or not so silently assigned to them.

To learn this lesson is to assume an attitude of transformational willingness and empowerment. It is a choice to see life in a different way, no longer to be a victim in relationships. To change our attitudes is to change our lives. Our attitudes determine our experiences and our world view. Our attitudes determine our success and our happiness. How much happiness is there in our lives? If we are not completely happy there is still something for us to learn. Maybe this is the time to start learning and growing once again.

As we go through this book, it is important to respect ourselves as well as those with whom we are not getting along. It is important that we do not sacrifice ourselves as martyrs or let ourselves be used as emotional punching bags. While these principles have shifted some cases of wife abuse in less than an hour, it is important to recognise whether or not we can handle certain situations. While most change indicated here is inner change (which leads to outer change), there are certain situations in which outer change is called for – to prevent abuse, for example. We must use our discernment to know the difference and to avoid remaining in physically threatening situations. These principles are here to empower us and to help us evolve. They are not here to be used to enslave ourselves further. If we give ourselves to these principles and use discernment, we will succeed.

Exercise

Today, make the choice for those you dislike to be on your team. Begin to see them as vital parts of your happiness. If they lose, the team loses. If they lose, you will have to pay the bill. Life is a team sport. There is no area where the interconnection of relationships is not a determining factor. They must win and you must win for there to be ultimate happiness.

If you believe someone must lose for you to win, you

will have to lose at least half the time to keep your win-lose attitude going in the game of life. You may not lose at this specific person's hands but you will lose in some fashion. It is time to learn how to be a great team player; a number of individuals playing together for a common goal can accomplish so much more than just one individual player. Make a new choice. Consistently playing win-win in spite of the behaviour of the person with whom you are not getting along advances your maturity and power. This is irresistible in the end, if not in the beginning.

As we grow in maturity, we first learn how to have successful relationships. Then we learn how to have a successful significant relationship. Finally we learn how to live, learn and work as part of a group. Your attitude and harmlessness are probably the two most significant aspects of your growth in maturity.

WAY 2 Trust Turns Everything to Advantage

When a problem occurs it is because our minds are split. The conscious mind wants to move forward but the subconscious mind is afraid of losing something to which we are attracted. We then project out the subconscious part onto some person or situation, which then seems to obstruct us. In truth, the obstruction is merely the objectification of our own ambivalence. This ambivalence shows itself as a lack of confidence.

Confidence turns problematic situations into merely 'something to handle'. It is trust that generates confidence. Trust involves choosing not to be naïve, a state in which we ignore information or intuition. Trust takes the entire situation in hand, no matter how seemingly negative, and begins to turn it to advantage. Trust, like faith, uses the power of our minds to begin to unfold a situation in a positive manner. Trust knows that no matter what the situation looks like, it is working for us. By knowing this, we can see every advantage and benefit in the situation.

Trust is the opposite of control or power struggle. It does not attempt to change anyone to meet our needs or to do it 'our way'. On the odd occasions that it is successful, when we win and people do things our way, they lose their attractiveness and go into sacrifice (see page 207). When they lose their attractiveness we also lose, and it begins to feel as if we are in sacrifice just being with them. When someone loses, they will typically bide their time until they can try to win and be on top again. Trust allows everyone to win. Trust is one of the primordial healing principles. There is no problem that trust cannot heal.

Exercise

Today, turn the power of your mind towards someone you dislike. When you begin to trust them and their actions, even acts that seem malicious begin, in a paradoxical sense, to work for you. Trust advances you and the situation.

As you begin to consider trusting someone with whom you are not getting along, you will probably notice feelings erupting, such as fear, anger or hurt. Trust whatever feelings arise in you. Even if they are negatives, they will begin to unfold positively. For example, if you are feeling fear and you put your trust into those feelings, they begin to change in a positive way. Trust your instincts. You may be guided to do something out of harms way. Negative emotions are not instinctive feelings, but reactions based on judgement. Trust unfolds them in a positive way.

Do not deny any feelings; be aware of them. Then imagine that you are sending your trust and the power of your mind through these feelings to both the person with whom you are not getting along and to the situation.

You may find that these emotions increase as you do this. This is a natural (but not necessary) part of the healing. Keep pouring your energy, the power of your trust, through these emotions to the person with whom you are not getting along until the feelings are gone and a sense of peace has come over you.

Any time you think of that person, send trust. You do not have to know how the situation could possibly get better in order to practise trust. Your only responsibility is to send your own trust until you feel at peace. You may feel yourself going through many layers of feelings. Once again, this is a healing process, and nothing to be worried about. If you don't experience layers of feelings, your healing will be even simpler.

Well applied, trust alone could totally transform this situation. At least three times today, and preferably any time you think of them, send trust to the person with whom you are not getting along until you feel peace.

WAY 3 See Those We Dislike in the Present Moment

The past is over. It doesn't exist, unless we keep it alive. The past we keep alive is a past that serves a purpose for us. It is a past we are using in a certain way to justify our behaviour in the present.

Letting go of the past frees us from its negative effects. Most of us do not live at all in the present, for if we did we would be happy. Living in the future means living in fear. Living in the past involves feelings of guilt and unworthiness. Any pain that we experience or negative emotions we feel are actually old pain or emotions that we have dragged into the present. When it seems to come up in the present, it is, in fact, old pain or upset triggered by something happening now.

These old patterns of pain are waiting to be unearthed and healed. To see someone in the present moment is to see them as if we were meeting them for the first time. We do not hold the past against them, and we are able to see them in a new light.

Also, for us to have a person with whom we are not getting along in our lives, means there is a pattern that was already present before we met them. This is still a way of dragging the past into the present. We bring any unfinished business we have with any significant persons from the past, such as parents, siblings, old lovers, etc., into our present relationships to be worked out. The mind keeps bringing in certain situations so that healing can finally occur.

If we have unresolved issues from the past we tend to perceive the present through the eyes of the past. This actually means we perceive 'through a glass darkly', behaving as if the way we see things is the way things are. Peace and happiness are the best indication that we are seeing things clearly without interference from the past.

Most of us are living in a present dictated by the past. The software of our bio-computer recapitulates the unfinished or unhealed past into the present over and over again. This does not leave us much in the way of new possibilities or choices. Our present is held hostage by our past. Only by leaving the past behind do we have a chance of being happy. It is only the past we are healing, or only our perception of the past that calls to be healed.

Exercise

Today, concentrate on seeing those you dislike in a new light, in the present. Even if you spend time with someone you dislike today, let each moment go as it passes and see only the present. Grievances are only about the past, never about the present.

Ask yourself what it is that bothers you about the person with whom you're not getting along. Who is it in your past that acted that way? Ask yourself if you would blame yourself for doing that same thing. If the answer is no, you will have freed everyone involved from the blame-guilt cycle that creates the problem.

If you cannot let the grievance go, ask yourself if you have ever behaved like this yourself. Ask yourself what you must have been feeling to act in that fashion. Would you blame yourself for that behaviour knowing what generated it?

If you have never acted in this fashion, ask yourself what you would have to be feeling to act in that way. Whatever feeling it would take for you to behave like that, you have probably felt before. Can you see what the person with whom you're not getting along must be feeling? You have known this feeling and how hard it was to experience. You understand this feeling. Could you blame anyone for this?

WAY 4 We are Using Those We Dislike to Avoid the Next Step

In any power struggle both sides are actually frightened to move forward, and so they fight to have things their way. They fight to gain control, 'knowing' their way is the best way. They are unwilling to consider how both sides are crucial for a new integration, a new answer. What's important to remember is that even if the one opposite us in a power struggle has an 'answer' that is absolutely wrong, the energy of that answer is, in fact, crucial to our success at the next step. And by taking that next step, rather than using those we dislike to avoid it, we will naturally integrate both sides into a successful new level.

We come into conflict with others when we try to get them to meet our needs, to do it our way. This creates competition, which in turn creates a delay, because we begin to believe that the other person is the source of our happiness. Winning becomes everything. But when we win a competition, we are then forced to carry the one who loses. The focus is on beating the other, rather than stepping forward where we could both could win equally.

The 'win-lose' attitude creates delay. Without a 'win-win' attitude, all of the dynamics of withdrawal, sabotage or a major attachment are at work, even if only on a subconscious level. Power struggle disguises the attachment, which blocks both intimacy and stepping forward. This attachment can be to a person, an old dream, a way of life or to anything we see as a source of our happiness. In a nutshell, it's anything that we are afraid to let go. But attachment can never satisfy us. First of all, our need for the attachment makes it exceptionally hard to succeed and impossible to receive. And if we do get what we need, we somehow feel disillusioned. It is not enough to satisfy us for long. Then we either seek a new attachment or feel desolate and disappointed. As we let go of our attachments we are naturally moved forward to a new level of receiving and success.

When we are frightened and lack courage, when we do not have the trust to say 'yes' to the next step, whatever it might be, it is convenient to have an excuse, a way in which no one could possibly blame us for not moving forward to a new level of maturity. Since we are caught in a terrible predicament with this 'offending' person, we do not have to face our fears. If we faced our fears and said 'yes' to the next step in trust, even if we do not know what that next step is, or what it will hold for us, we would move forward into a new level of partnership and maturity for all involved, and a new level of success for all concerned.

Exercise

Today, just ask yourself what attachment it is that you are holding onto – which led to this conflict – and see what pops into your head. If nothing pops in, it is because it is so obvious that you do not consider it, or it is too well defended to see. Spend some time dwelling on this theme to see what emerges.

An attachment exchanges glamour or glitter for what really would make us happy. It is always something outside us that we use as a crutch in order to have certain needs met. But fulfilment comes from what you give and receive, not from what you take or get. Examine today if this attachment is really making you happy.

Be willing to avoid using someone with whom you don't get along as an excuse or reason for avoiding the step forward. Be willing to not hide your fear of the next step in intimacy. Choose to step forward. Say 'yes' to the next step, and await the new level that will come to you. It will be better for you and for everyone.

When you are aware of the attachment be willing to let it go to move forward.

WAY 5   Forgive to Heal this Problem

Many people are afraid to forgive because forgiving is associated with being a victim. We are afraid that if we give in, and forgive, the person with whom we are in conflict will continue to do what they are doing. Yet, forgiveness is not about giving in. It is forgiveness that changes perception and experience; it changes the very pattern that initiated the problem. Forgiveness is not sacrifice; it equates with transformation and peace.

What you hold against those you dislike is a judgement and a grievance. Yet, only the guilty blame others. The innocent see nothing to condemn. When we feel guilty, we attempt to avoid suffering. We repress the feeling and project it out on to someone else. Thus, what we hold against others reflects exactly what we are judging in ourselves. Our grievances and projections on others give us access to finding areas of conflict inside ourselves that have somehow stopped us. We can work very hard in our lives to hide these buried subconscious elements, which act as an invisible barrier to hold us back. Yet, all the hard work of compensating to hide our guilt is unrewarded. Only giving allows us to receive. Compensations to prove you are good go unrewarded.

Our forgiveness of others releases our buried guilt. So, rather than make someone you dislike be the scapegoat and lose the opportunity to heal hidden conflicts, today choose to do something that will free you both. If you continue to judge, you will be stuck with exactly the same characteristics that you detest in others and you will remain in the same situation. Your guilt, although hidden, will continue to punish you.

A fight, judgement, or grievance locks us into the very behaviour we hate. Whatever the person with whom we're not getting along is doing, we must see it as a call for help. If we learn to respond to the needs of others, our leadership abilities and confidence grow.

When we become distressed, we are alerted to an error that we are making in our present situation. It is a sign of resistance and instead of continuing to resist, we can view the fact that we are resistant as a signal that forgiveness is needed. Judging others' behaviour locks us into doing the very thing we judge, or it locks us into an opposite role that is, ultimately, only compensatory. Again, such roles do not allow us to receive and therefore increase feelings of deadness and burnout.

Forgiveness protects our rights and our freedom while releasing the illusion of subconscious guilt. Forgiveness transforms a situation by transforming perception. Forgiveness reinstates everyone's innocence, including our own.

Exercise

List three grievances you have with another person. For each one ask yourself: Would I hold this against myself? If the answer is no, you are both free. If the answer is 'yes', consider that what you hold against them you will also hold against yourself and those you love. Given this, would you like to choose again?

Turn the forgiveness over to the part of your mind that has all the answers – your higher mind. Any time you think of someone you dislike, be aware that the forgiveness is being handled for you. Enjoy the results.

While forgiveness may be extremely difficult for you, you can use heaven's power to succeed. State with each grievance, 'I forgive you and myself, through God's love.'

WAY 6 Life is About Happiness and Healing

Life is about happiness and joy. But happiness is also as elusive as a butterfly and if we chase it, we'll scare it away. Sitting quietly or following our true purpose allows happiness to come to us naturally. Happiness comes out of love and creativity. It comes out of the fulfilment of living our personal purpose and being part of the world's evolution. When we are not happy, we can use its absence as an indicator of something that we are called upon to heal, learn and change. Healing, learning and changing bring about the conditions needed for happiness.

Let us look at our bad relationships again. If we are not happy in a situation with another, we are probably caught in a chronic painful pattern. When we experience a grievance, it is typically a part of a pattern that began with someone in our childhood, or with our families. What we are experiencing now began a long time ago and the strength of the upset speaks of how long it has been with us. Forgiving the original family member helps to make the present forgiveness and healing easy. In most cases, we have not forgiven a family member for something that we believed they did not do or, on the other hand, something they did do.

It's important to look at this from another angle.

What they did not do or provide for us is a key indication of something that we were called to provide – a gift (see page 206). If we had given the gift, there would be no grievance and no situation requiring forgiveness. In this situation, we would have seen a problem for which we had a gift (the answer), and having failed to give it, we blamed ourselves and then went into sacrifice to try to make it better. This sets up the first line of defences, ostensibly to cover our guilt, which was a mistake in the first place.

Rather than being able to transform a situation by offering our gift, we ultimately 'catch' the same problem pattern, and it is this that continues to generate guilt, lack of self-worth and valuelessness now. These feelings may be subconscious, but the very fact that we have continuing grievances is evidence that they exist.

These feelings of valuelessness require us to 'do', to stay busy and to work hard to hide and compensate because valuelessness always ultimately leads to death temptations. Yet, this situation can be simply removed by asking to be carried back to our centre by our higher mind and then allowing the grace of the gift we had come to give to be given. It is our family trap that turned into a conspiracy against ourselves that generates relationship and victim problems.

Either guilt or blame exaggerates our self-importance, which is a compensation for feeling valueless. To be in our centre and to let our higher mind work from within re-establishes our value and allows creativity to flow. Trying to force creativity lessens or hampers it. Being creative lets it flow through us and

gives us joy. Either guilt or blame puts an un-
wholesome compensating attention on us that negates
the sense of ease that is one of the main qualities of
happiness and peace. Our egos always want to video
the best profile of us fighting against all odds.

Any sign of difficulty in our lives is a sign that we
are pushing and trying to accomplish something, and
get ego recognition and untrue attention. Pushing,
busyness and difficulty are all signs of hidden guilt
and of acting in a positive way without reward to
hide feelings of failure. These types of things show
that we have hidden guilt and a compensation (see
page 205) going on, which means that we are not
receiving the reward for all the work. It simply results
in attention for ourselves, which is a sign of hidden
guilt and defensive compensation. Blaming someone
locks us into sacrifice because of our judgement.
What we judge we are stuck with, as if it's true. We
act righteously but feel imprisoned and put upon by
a bad situation. This also gives us the glamour, the
untrue attention and self-centredness of the victim,
an inability to recognise our part in it, and the guilt
that consequently remains hidden and unexpurgated
in us. To hold onto blame keeps us locked in guilt,
which keeps us from moving forward and keeps us
finding ways to punish ourselves.

Now the next major dynamic to examine is the fear
of moving forward that this hidden or not so hidden
guilt supports. Forgiving ourselves and others naturally moves us forward. Guilt and blame support stag-
nation – being stuck in a situation where we are not
and can never be happy. One purpose of guilt and

blame is to avoid moving forward and facing that which frightens us.

Fear of the future is another way to place undue emphasis on ourselves. Undue emphasis will support a glamour, which is something that glitters but is not gold and takes the form of either an exaggerated personality or disappointment and shame. Any area in which we are not succeeding is an area we are actually succeeding in getting some subconscious agendas met, which are more important to us than our success. These other agendas are to make up for the past and are hidden forms of getting rather than receiving or succeeding.

Glamour, which is an untrue way of seeking and being in the spotlight, hides a place of future disappointment because it is based on comparison, which leads to shame and pain sooner or later. Happiness and creativity place no undue emphasis on ourselves, but allow everything to be in a right relationship. Our personal purpose allows us to see our part in the world plan so we may see ourselves as part of the whole, a thread in the fabric without the undue emphasis that leads to pain. Glamour is a mistaken attempt to make up for pain and needs from the past by getting attention from others. This leads to a self-consciousness that is the opposite of leadership, flow, spontaneity and enjoyment.

Lastly, if we are afraid of moving forward it is because we are afraid to lose something that we are holding on to. Therefore, behind any disagreement with others is an indulgence that we are holding onto and have probably outgrown. Our disagreements hide some attachment that we believed would make us happy, although it hasn't, the result being an almost continual state of sacrifice.

In most cases, these indulgences or 'somethings' that we cling to are something outside us – something we believe will make us happy if we can only achieve them. These are attachments that we think will emotionally save us and make us happy. These 'somethings' become a sort of idol and although we may achieve fleeting happiness, there will ultimately be disappointment. For in reality, the only path to happiness is from within. Attachments may be relationships, success at work, financial success, or something less tangible. Whatever their source, they will not bring happiness, although all of these 'somethings' can be achieved naturally and gracefully when we are happy.

Today it is time to truly examine what we might be holding onto, for it is this that keeps us from stepping forward.

Each step forward we take allows a few more personalities to melt away, and our love and creativity to shine through. This is really the love and creativity of heaven shining through us, gracing us and those around us. When we do something self-consciously and personally, our actions are undertaken by our personalities, which are self-concepts that appeared when we lost bonding. In this case, we never truly receive, but only indulge. Indulgence is only half of a vicious indulgence-sacrifice circle. Feeding one demands a feeding for the other.

Exercise

Today, examine the situation again. What is being called for? Forgiveness? Centring? Taking the next step? Letting go?

Whatever it is, it is not something for you to do. Do not trade in one problem for another. Ask your higher mind to complete what needs to be done. Your higher mind can do it for you, through you. Do whatever you are inspired or guided to do. Do not hold yourself back by exaggerating yourself positively or negatively. If you are not in your own way, happiness comes to you.

WAY 7 Our Anger is a Form of Control

Anger is a form of control. It is an attempt to force others to act how we want them to act, to meet our needs in the situation by doing it our way. This makes us feel secure and comfortable.

Anger is a form of attack that we feel is justified because someone else has seemingly attacked first – by doing, or not doing something. In response, we feel justified in attacking. But anger is a defence, which hides deeper feelings like guilt, hurt, fear or sadness, with which we do not want to deal. Anger keeps a situation in power struggle and therefore it is an avoidance of something that would resolve the situation.

Anger makes the statement that we are perfectly justified in feeling and acting this way because another is to blame for our feelings. This form of immaturity blocks the ability to listen, learn, receive and change.

Our anger may show itself in different forms. It may show as direct attack, passive aggression, withdrawal, complaining or suffering. All of these forms are an attempt to gain control rather than a means to learn from the situation at hand and change. Even if your anger succeeded in controlling, it still only puts off a valuable lesson that wants and needs to be learned. Putting off a lesson allows it to become a trial later, while learning the lesson now leads to greater confidence. Lack of confidence leads to control and anger in its many forms.

Anger always hides some degree of a fear of loss so that we again feel justified in our attack. Anger also hides a need onto which we want to hold, and have satisfied. We would rather fight than surrender this hidden attachment we think will bring us happiness. Yet attachment only leads to pain or disappointment and has the power to subvert what is true. Our attachments hide a need that tries to take but cannot receive. It often leads us into situations where we get hurt because we are giving only to take. This form of vampirism will cause us to be pushed away, which then leads to both hurt and anger.

Our anger does not allow us to step forward because we are trying to change outside situations through control. This method will never be truly effective, no matter how well we have mastered the art of controlling others. When we have won the control game with a partner, for example, their loss causes them to appear unattractive to us, which is, of course, a loss for us.

To significantly and truly change the world around us, we must change our minds. By doing this at a subconscious level, it would mean that a person or a situation changes without any need for us to control or dominate.

Controlling means believing we have the answer for what is 'best'. And anger means that we think we know the answer. At best, this viewpoint is misinformed and at worst, ludicrous. We have only to look at our own 'track record' for happiness to realise how much we do not know about what is in our best interest.

Our ability to see the whole picture is limited, especially in regard to ourselves. Even our visionaries see only a slice of the whole. Yet there is that part of our minds that, if not limited by our personalities and needs, can inspire us with answers and unfold the situation well beyond our normal thinking.

Exercise

Today, be willing to recognise that your anger just does not work. Take a step in maturity, a step towards seeing that anger is never justified and that pardon always is.

Visualise yourself making the choice to step forward where both your needs and other people's needs can be met in a whole new way. Visualise yourself as stepping forward to a new level of success. Feel the confidence that comes with stepping forward to a new level. None of us knows what this step looks like until we step forward, but when we step forward things are always better.

You can use the person with whom you're not getting along as a gauge to know how much healing is still required inside you, rather than using them as an excuse to fight to avoid moving forward. Even if the person with whom you're not getting along engages in stupid and malicious acts, your anger locks you into their level and reality, and denies you your opportunity for growth and learning. Your anger is a reaction that imprisons you. Instead, you can maintain a responsive poise as you generate the harmlessness that is always the heart of your continued evolution and sustained happiness and joy.

WAY 8 Our Anger Hides Deeper Feelings

Anger is a defensive feeling meant to protect deeper feelings, such as hurt, guilt, deadness, fear, insecurity and frustration. Anger falls away if we allow ourselves to understand and experience the deeper feeling, instead of attacking or withdrawing. If we become interested in knowing ourselves, we can choose an attitude of being willing to experience our more primordial emotions and resolve them.

Wanting to know and understand the emotions buried within us involves a step of integrity. We have been carrying them for many years, expending energy on them and not always keeping them under control. They always lead us into situations where they become triggered in order to be resolved. We then have an important choice to make. Either we use the situation as an opportunity to learn and heal, thus being open to much greater learning and success, or we use our feelings as justification for attacking another. Only those who blame themselves accuse or attack others. The healed and innocent have no need to obstruct their learning and growth in this fashion.

As we begin to discover the emotions inside us, we begin to discover our self-defeating patterns. As we discover our self-defeating patterns, we find our self-concepts. Self-concepts are either positive or negative.

Positive self-concepts are compensations for how negative we feel about ourselves. They try to prove we are really good people. But the extent to which we are caught up in proving our goodness, is the extent to which our negative self-concepts are implied. What we try to prove we do not fully believe.

Our negative self-concepts are also trying to prove something. They are out to prove that we are not truly good or powerful or children of God. They defend beliefs in our own guilt and evil. They are also a compensation (see page 205) at a much deeper level that hides our true goodness and wholeness. When people are out to prove how bad they are, it is because they are afraid of the responsibility of true goodness. Or they are afraid of being powerful and having it all, or even afraid to admit they are a child of God.

Any compensation is a defence that does not allow for reward or receiving. Any negative belief or guilt about ourselves calls for a self-punishment, which is sometimes experienced as outside attack. No one can attack us unless we have personal guilt and seek to obviate it through attack by others.

Whenever we are attacked or victimised by outside forces in an attempt to pay off guilt, we feel bad (a description of guilt) about being victimised. So the very thing we use to pay off our guilt actually increases it. Defences do not work, which is why it is important to find our buried painful emotions and take responsibility for them so we can heal them.

The person with whom we are not getting along can be the very person who can help us find these painful, self-defeating attitude patterns and emotions, if we choose not to get caught in reactive, self-righteous patterns. But again, the extent of our self-righteousness is the extent to which we are hiding guilt feelings. Otherwise, why the need to act so right? A positive self-concept, especially a role, hides a negative self-concept, while a negative self-concept hides our true goodness.

Exercise

Be aware of any forms of anger today: aggression, withdrawal, passive aggression, suffering and any form of victimisation. Be willing to experience whatever buried feelings there are underneath the anger. Ask yourself how old those feelings are and how old you were when these feelings began. Ask yourself about the pattern or compensation that has existed around these emotions. Ask yourself what self-concepts you have about yourself (positive or negative) that these emotions have supported. Make new decisions about these self-concepts using truth as your guide.

You might want to do this exercise in columns to make it clearer to you.

Form of positive anger?	Buried feelings?	How old?	What pattern or compensation?	What self-concepts?	What aspects do these feelings hide?

WAY 9 Communication – The Bridge of Healing

Because communication leads to forgiveness, it is the heart of healing. About eighty-five per cent of all conflict seems to be healed by clarification of what we are experiencing – in other words our intentions and goals in the situation. The other fifteen per cent represents areas of chronic conflict for both parties that have now surfaced to be healed. Fighting for our way, overtly or covertly, does not lead to either maturity or progress. While it is important not to let ourselves be overrun, fighting suggests a weakened, fearful and immature position.

Communication is the bridge between two parties, on which both can win in a mature and more integrated fashion. The first aspect of communication is the willingness to set a goal in which both parties can win, and not stop before the empowering goal is reached by both. If there is a sense of sacrifice or compromise (which indicates the communication has not come to resolution), eventually one or both parties will feel that they have lost, and the conflict will resume.

There are a number of safeguards to maintain effective communication. The first is to be discerning rather than naive. It is important not give ourselves over and be used in any situation, to be aware when someone is using our 'niceness' against us in a manipulative way or if someone is 'vampiring' the communication to take and use our energy. Most people do this unconsciously and are willing to stop as they become aware of this subtle form of attack. But if we become aware someone holds no good intention for us, it might be necessary to remove ourselves from the situation. We need to step forward in our healing and consciousness, letting them go rather than falling for the glamour of trying to save them (and thus becoming an enabler), or giving ourselves up to be used in sacrifice.

We can also realistically address how successful we have been in our healing process. For example, how much has the relationship improved? Do we feel freer in their company? Less burdened? How much better do we feel about them and about ourselves when we are in their company?

It is important not to give ourselves over to abuse in the name of healing. On the other hand, we can discern what can be overlooked in the name of healing and maturity on our parts. We need to examine how sensitive we are and how quickly we take offence. We can make new choices regarding our behaviour and set new goals for ourselves and our relationships.

Next, if we wish to be successful, it is important to communicate willingness to learn and change (the purpose of our communication is to change ourselves rather than others). Our change will naturally facilitate change in others. Deliberately tying to change others will strengthen their resistance and changes the nature of the reason why change is being made.

For if we force or manipulate them to change, we are only doing so to meet our own needs. We are never in a conflict unless there is something to learn and to heal.

The next step in communication is to make clear what is not working or what it is we are upset about. Recognising we are never upset for the reason we think allows us to reassure our partners in this communication. The purpose of our communication is not to trigger their guilt, but to come to resolution. If we then 'own' what is not working by taking responsibility for our experiences, we inspire our partners with a willingness to continue communication now and in the future. They understand that the purpose of the communication is not to make them wrong.

To do this, we recognise our experiences as being our responsibilities, and then share our underlying feelings and experiences as clearly as we can. Next, we become aware of how a particular feeling or situation is actually part of a pattern that began for us in an earlier time and place. Then we share this with the person with whom we are in conflict. If we share our process as we become aware of it, keeping to the emotional content as much as possible, we will find the communication shifts us and moves us forward.

Also, our willingness to receive their communication, even if they are not playing by our principles, can produce great movement. Anyone who feels they are heard becomes very receptive. What makes this successful, even if our communication partner is attacking us, is our willingness to not defend ourselves, our willingness to remain harmless. For this to be successful, we must be willing to experience negative or painful feelings that may arise in us and in our attackers. Realise that these feelings did not just begin recently, but were there within us for some time. They're coming up as an opportunity for us to heal them just by experiencing the feelings until they are gone. This might even take a day or two, but once it is finished, that layer of pain will be finished forever. If we pour love into someone while they are having a tantrum, they are unlikely to act quite like that again.

It takes courage to face our own feelings in order to heal and evolve, because we don't want to feel pain. Unfortunately, much of our learning and evolution does take place in this manner. Our willingness to learn in these types of situations can progress us to a point where we do not shy away from our pain, but use it as a barometer for healing. Taking this stance eventually takes away the need to learn with pain as the teacher. In other words, we don't need to learn the hard way.

All kinds of emotions may be triggered in this communication, such as guilt, fear, hurt, loss, need, anger and frustration. But to use the situation to experience our feelings and communicate them until they are gone, re-associates us with our feelings and ourselves. The extent to which we do this allows for partnership, receiving and eventually the transcendence of negative emotion into joy and the higher mental and spiritual realms. But we cannot avoid negative emotions. We must heal or transcend them to move forward.

To have a successful relationship we must have successful communication. It is an essential factor in maturity and evolution. So, we might as well decide to become an expert in communication for it will benefit our love lives, our careers and our families.

Exercise

Today, decide to become an expert on communication. It will serve you throughout your whole life. Practise the principles of communication in this lesson with those around you. You may want to write them down so that they are available to you.

Practise these principles especially with someone you dislike. Let them know you value the relationship enough to communicate to make it better. Appreciate their willingness to work with you. If they are totally uncooperative, you can ask someone close to you to role-play them. Have them just 'tune in' to the person you dislike, paying special attention to that person's emotional experience as they communicate.

As you imagine them in front of you, communicate what is not working for you and take responsibility for what you are feeling. While you are sharing and as it surfaces, experience and follow the feeling, and/or life pattern back to the time and place where it began. If no pattern emerges about where this painful feeling or conflict began, just acknowledge your responsibility for it. Describe, as best you can, the nuances of this feeling; for example, how it feels; what it is like to feel this; the thoughts that come with it; how it affects you, etc. Imagine yourself sharing the feeling about this with the person with whom you're not getting along. To keep it transformative, stay as close to the heart of the feeling as possible in your sharing without getting caught up in thoughts or stories.

Above all, make a choice to take a step forward. Take quiet time for yourself, and you will find the guidance you need.

WAY 10 Our Grievances Hide Unfinished Business from within the Family

Any unfinished business that was within our families as we grew up will be brought into our present relationships. It has long been known in therapeutic circles that bosses and authority figures 'take the heat' for unfinished business with fathers and mothers. At this point in our lives, we may consciously feel quite different about the parent with whom we had the original problem. But if there is buried judgement, pain or guilt, it will tend to show up again in our present situations, where there is a chance of getting the old pain out and transmitted.

The people we don't get along with now are actually helping us to deal with some unfinished business with a family member. If we realise there is a pattern involved, it will serve to lessen the attack we make on others. Then we can bring our attention back to the only place where the problem can really be healed, which is inside ourselves. If we take responsibility for this conflict in our lives, our sense of responsibility can change the situation.

Even if nothing readily comes to mind about a conflict from our original family (that which is subconscious does not always readily lend itself to consciousness), we must be willing to examine our lives and our patterns of relationships. Do present feelings rekindle feelings that have arisen in the past?

The present situation is an excellent opportunity to heal the pattern, to avoid compounding any existing patterns and certainly to avoid beginning any new problem patterns that will later have to be cleared up. This situation serves as an excellent opportunity for healing, lessening our inner conflict and stress, and graduating us to a new level of consciousness.

Exercise

Imagine that someone you dislike is standing in front of you. Imagine now that what you see is actually only an unlikeable costume and if you pulled off the mask, the person with whom you had the original conflict would appear. Now, reach over to the person and pull off the mask . . . Who is there? Ask this person: 'How may I help you?'

Endeavour to accomplish the essence of this request for the person, first in your imagination and then in life, especially as it serves both of your interests. If in the rare case their request seems destructive, keep asking them the purpose of their request until you get to the very essence.

Ask yourself the following questions and trust what 'pops' into your mind. You may not receive the exact facts by this method but you will at least be shown the pattern involved.

If you were to know when this problem began (that is currently showing itself as a conflict with the person you are

*not getting along with), it was probably when you were
at the age of_____.*

*If you were to know who was involved when this problem
began it was probably_____*

*If you were to know what had occurred to begin this prob-
lem for you it was probably_____*

*This problem represents a place where you are off your
centre. This problem is a place where you lack balance
and peace. To return to your centre, which is a place of
peace, innocence and grace, and to restore your bonding,
ask your higher mind to carry you back to the centre you
lost, and to carry all of the people in the original situation back to their centres. Finally, ask that your higher
mind allows grace to flow to everyone in the original situation. If the situation is not completely shifted to one of
peace, ask your higher mind to carry you back to a second
centre, and to more centres if needed.*

*This centring exercise puts an end to the psychological
pattern, as well as its incumbent guilt, valuelessness, sacrifice, grievance and the unrequited need and suffering cycle
that such a pattern represents.*

WAY 11 Someone We Dislike is Our Projection

This lesson is of special appeal to those who have a deep interest in growth, change and transformation. The principle is really a willingness to see everyone and everything that happens as a learning situation. It requires a willingness to see everyone and every situation as a projection of our subconscious mind and, at times, our unconscious mind. As this makes the outer world a reflection of the inner mind, the outer world can be changed by changing our mind within.

If we remember that each person we see outside ourselves actually represents a part of our mind that has been judged, fragmented, dis-identified, buried and projected outward, then we can be much more ready and willing to do the work to win these pieces of ourselves back. We can do this through integrating the missing or repressed parts.

Many people are frightened of integrating parts of themselves they are projecting onto others because they are afraid of bringing in what appear to be negative elements. However, the act of integration provides an inoculation or vaccination against further negativity of the same type. Through this integration we learn the lesson that is being provided, and then progress on to the next lesson, the next projection, the next step, the next challenge.

There are some people with whom we have only 'chance', short encounters. There are others with whom we have lessons that go on for a while and seem to end (the majority of relationships fall into this category). Then there are those unique relationships where people are close enough to our own level of development where there are unlimited lessons of growth that continue to unfold. The people in our families are typically people with whom our lessons may unfold continuously and with whom we may have one of those rare lifetime learning situations. People typically continue in relationships for as long as they can, and when no more can be learned at a given time that learning situation ends. Our closest relationships, especially family relationships, represent parts of our soul we want to win back and integrate in this life. They can represent chronic problems or gifts, all of which frightened us, so that we judged and projected out only to those closest to us. We have now come to win these parts back so that we both share the gifts. What we judged becomes benign in and with both of us.

We can do much in our lives for ourselves and the world at large because we never learn just for ourselves. There is no lesson we learn that does not improve the world. We can do much for everyone by becoming a willing and happy learner. Where fear and judgement are healed, where projections are pulled and transformed so that others around us seem to grow, it is evident not only to ourselves but to everyone.

This process begins when we see no one's interest as separate from our own. It is furthered through such forms of healing as understanding, acceptance, giving, forgiving, letting go, trust, communication, integration, commitment, truth, receiving, grace and responsiveness. It is hindered through fear, guilt, suffering, pain, selfishness, evil, authority conflict, control, hurt, grievance, need and all of the things that seem to generate and be generated by separateness.

Exercise

Imagine that someone you dislike is standing before you, but instead of seeing their body or personality, you see the trillions of light particles that make up their being. Experience this glowing sentient light as their essence.

Now see yourself in the same way.

Next, imagine these two lights are joining together. As they completely join, see yourself emerging in a whole new way with a great deal more confidence. See and feel yourself as having integrated and thus dispersed the negative qualities, while accentuating and multiplying the many positive ones that come with integration.

To develop the ability to heal by integrating projections, try this helpful metaphor. Imagine that the whole world is a video game and the video game is a reflection of our minds. In this video game world, it is only we who exist (it is a one person game). At some ancient, primeval time a spell was cast on us that created an illusion; where all that was in Oneness seemed to shatter into billions and billions of separate entities. Our mission, when we choose to accept it, is to reverse the spell and begin to reunite all of the seemingly separate entities into a whole. How well is your game going?

WAY 12 Our Grievances Hide Our Guilt

This is an important lesson, for it is guilt that keeps us in sacrifice. It is guilt that creates all forms of suffering. This is the guilt that comes from any unfinished business of the past, anything about which we feel bad. This is the guilt that causes conflict because only the self-deceived could be in conflict. We live in a world of conflict, self-deception and illusion about what is truly valuable.

Since guilt is such an uncomfortable feeling, we typically deny it, hide it and project it out on others. We can only accuse others of misdemeanours of which we are ourselves guilty. We can only judge those on whom we project our own unfinished and hidden conflicts. That is why recognising our innocence is so important both for ourselves and others. Innocence could free us of pain, scarcity and the separation generated by conflicts. It could literally save the world.

The grievances we have are one of the best ways to hide guilt. Our grievances keep us in a reactive rather than a responsive mode. Our grievances allow us to scapegoat and to avoid looking for the real solutions within ourselves. Grievances that come from inner conflicts and guilt promote outer conflicts. Again, we literally accuse others of what is buried in our subconscious or unconscious mind. To live a life of no-fault relationships, a life in which we are doing the best we can (given inner and outer circumstances, beliefs and stress), yet know we can all do better, is to put the responsibility of our emotions and life back into our own hands. It would be an empowering way to live, both for ourselves and for those around us.

We can use our grievances and conflict as a way to discover the source or roots of our hidden conflicts and guilt. Resolving these inner conflicts and guilt is a very easy way to resolve outer problems and conflicts. Properly used, our grievances can be a way to find guilt that is so well buried we would have no other way of finding it. Your grievances can assist you to heal yourself in spite of denial, because your grievances point to your guilt.

When people have grievances they feel righteous, and righteousness is really just a cover for feelings of 'wrongfulness' or guilt. We could take this opportunity with anyone with whom we're not getting along and begin to search for our hidden guilt. We could use every grievance as the first step in finding our guilt and, through forgiveness, declaring our own and others' innocence. As we judge, so shall we be judged. The only working solution is forgiveness and working for everyone's innocence, everyone's interests.

Exercise

Think of a particular grievance you have. Spend time now 'owning' that particular behaviour pattern as if it were yours, albeit subconsciously. Notice how you treat yourself as if you were doing it all the time. Really experience the feeling that this generates until there is no longer an emotional charge on it. Do this until you can say: 'Yes, this is me. I'm just like this.' Now dwell on this behaviour until you can begin to feel innocent about this behaviour.

WAY 13 A Power Struggle is a Place Where Everyone Eventually Loses

Power struggles, especially those in relationships, have no winners. If we win, the other person goes into the losing position. From the losing position they also lose what attractiveness they have, and they typically enter into a sacrifice position. Either way, when someone around us loses, we end up paying the bill, or it is only a matter of time before they seek to ambush us and regain domination.

In a power struggle at least one of the parties feels bad. Because they feel bad, they look around for someone to blame.

This does not solve the problem, even if we seem to win. When human beings are in emotional pain they tend to react, run or attack each other. Being aware of how we react in response to pain helps to keep us from displacing onto those around us, or from 'unloading' our emotional baggage when someone strikes out at us. When we are aware, we realise that peoples' behaviours express either a call for love or a call for help. People act in certain ways because of the way they feel. If they are acting in a way that generates pain, it is because they are in pain. Being responsive to their pain and their needs allows us to communicate without locking us into a fight or conflict. It allows us to assume a leadership position rather than being trapped by the situation.

No one wants to feel pain, and it takes a great deal of maturity not to react when we are in pain or when someone has struck out at us. But it is possible, and it allows us to transform and unfold situations in positive ways. It is a sign of maturity. Even while we are in pain and tempted to react and strike out, we can ask ourselves: What would help the situation? If we listen, we will notice that a way is intuitively being suggested to us. If we respond according to the quiet voice within, we will find the situation unfolding positively. If we choose to move forward rather than strike back, our healing and our lives can take a step forward.

Exercise

Today, turn any power struggle away from its ability to stop your forward movement. Turn it into a situation of growth. If you are in a power struggle, listen to the voice from your higher mind. If you are experiencing any kind of problem today, listen to your higher mind. Take five minutes to ask and listen for the solution. The solution is always being offered if you have the willingness to hear. Of course, one of the greatest arts is to be able to achieve this listening in the midst of your pain.

Once you see the possibility of having everyone in the situation win, it will occur and you will be inspired by the results. Being willing to change adds to your ability to receive, succeed and love.

WAY 14 Those We Dislike are Not Holding Us Back

Those we dislike are not holding us back – we are responsible. As a matter of fact, the extent to which we think that someone else is holding us back is the extent to which we are using others to hold back ourselves. The only true conspiracy against us is self-conspiracy.

It takes a great deal of maturity to realise that everything happens for the best. Many of us go through major lessons, challenges, trials and tests throughout our lifetimes. A trial is just an unlearned lesson that is now coming round to be learned. A test is a major opportunity. It could actually be a life or death situation or a situation where we would feel crushed if we do not pass the test. To pass the test is similar to passing an initiation in that we springboard forward in consciousness. Our difficult relationships are providing such opportunities.

If life is about the expansion of consciousness so we might grow in love and joy, then this is just an opportunity to transform ourselves and move to a whole new level. If we think those we dislike are holding us back, then we have some other idea of what life and happiness is all about. We hold other values, attitudes or hidden agendas to gain love, joy and happiness. Actually, we work hard for so many things that in the end do not even satisfy us, much less give us love, happiness and joy. What gives us joy is love, creativity, giving, receiving, forgiveness and living our purpose. In giving and receiving there is a natural flow forward. Forgiveness ends fear and conflict and creates the vital change needed for movement towards joy and happiness.

Many times in life we come to important crossroads. We can choose either to continue to make the same choices and move in the same direction we have always done, or to make a significant step in a new direction. Forgiveness allows for that significant step. The willingness to change and not use others to hold us back takes new direction. After the initial turmoil that change can sometimes bring, we are raised to a whole new level of confidence by stepping forward. It is these changes that keep us flexible, vital and alive. Someone with whom we are not getting along shows a rigid, defended place of hidden pain. When you see someone like this, use the opportunity to help them and thus help yourself.

Not to choose transformation in the face of our problems is to dig in our heels and try to get the rest of the world to change for us. It did not work for us as children and it will not work for us as adults. Adult tantrums that take the form of anger and aggression, or feeling hurt and attacked, are no more successful than our childhood tantrums.

Exercise

Now is the time to choose to take a significant step forward. Now is the time to be willing to leap forward to a new level. Now is the time that forgiveness will change your perception and increase your learning.

Give yourself some quiet time to listen for inspiration. You will always be guided to help make the situation better unless you have a vested interest in hiding something. Follow your inspirations, because the solution will allow everyone to win; you won't waste time obsessing about the situation and you won't ignore it when it needs to be handled.

Those We Dislike Have
Come to Help

Those we dislike are here to help, and only our attitudes or perspectives signal otherwise. Let us start by saying that our general purpose in life is similar to everyone's: love, happiness, abundance, joy and evolution. Then comes the question of how one achieves this.

Let us say someone we dislike is over-sensitive, cantankerous and aggressive. Our thought is: If I want to be happy I must stay away from this person, because every time I am around them they say or do something that upsets me, and I am not happy anymore. This attitude, which may ultimately be true, will not further our happiness or our maturity if we do not first apply some basic principles to help the situation evolve. First of all, we are not placed in a situation in which there is no answer. As impossible as some situations seem, there is always an answer where everyone can win. Secondly, we are not where we are by accident, but by design. We are in this situation because there is some vital lesson in it for us to learn. We may as well learn it now.

This situation points to a long-standing conflict within ourselves. Without someone to project this conflict onto, it might have taken years for us to get in touch with why we just are not happy. If that person were gone we would still have the conflict inside that defies our best efforts at happiness and we would not know why. Our pain is the beginning of the healing process. It lets us know of a place where we need healing, a place where we are not harmless (a place where we choose not to harm, attack, seek revenge or be a victim, which is a hidden form of attack). Do not lose this opportunity, for you will only have to face it later.

To begin working with the problem, it is important not to shy away from the painful feelings. They are helpful indicators of some buried conflict. As we follow the painful feelings, they can lead us to where our conflicts are buried. Our outward conflicts are just indications of conflicts within. All conflicts stem from doubt or lack of self-confidence and all doubt is really self-doubt. Self-doubt stems from wanting two different things or having conflicting wishes. Having conflicting wishes makes it impossible to move forward, as there is a fear of losing one of the wishes. That is why all healing has to do with some form of integration of the two conflicting wishes.

Your conflict with the person with whom you're not getting along just points to a place of denial or self-deception that has been revealed. To further deny it by attacking them merely compounds the problem. We must acknowledge this conflict as our own. This is the beginning of healing. To attack and fight the person with whom we're not getting along is to use them as the whipping boy for something else that is disturbing us. And fighting will not make us happy. Attack does not bring us joy. Joy arises out of love and joining and the healing that allows it. Happiness is its natural by-product. Attack thoughts and grievances come out of the righteousness that hides self-blame.

Dynamically, there are only two feelings, love and fear. All other feelings stem from them. Anything that is not love is fear. Fear is generated from our attack thoughts which we then project out onto the world. We then become frightened of a menacing world, not realising that it began with our thoughts. This then opens us up to greater negative influences.

To become happy we must take the stance of love. To begin with this may be a stance of harmlessness and then forgiveness. If we are not happy then we are not harmless. It would take our choice to become harmless, or our choice to forgive, for success and happiness to occur. If we are not happy, the only way to become happy is to heal. Healing comes from forgiveness, trust, integration, understanding, acceptance, commitment, letting go, etc., and not from running away or winning battles by being right. These only cover the conflict which will, at some point, have to be revisited to be healed.

All conflicts stem from old broken hearts. All conflicts stem from unmet needs, and our needs are expressions of fear, demand and attack. Our needs are not only met but transcended through our forgiveness, our giving forth of the very thing we think we need.

Our present conflicts come from old grievances. Grievances come from situations where people did not do what we wanted them to do. They did not meet our needs but did what they did to meet their needs. These needs and grievances are carried through life until we choose a place of healing. If we hold grievances like this, we will either be doing what they did to people around us or overcompensating against this pattern and wasting a great deal of energy.

When chronic needs and grievances are carried through life, they typically become a tantrum. These tantrums are places people are really crying for help and love. Tantrums are typically a situation in which the child inside the adult body is wounded. But where someone close to us upsets us with their tantrum it points to a hidden tantrum on our part. Let us find and heal the wounded children in us so we don't hold others hostage to our pain. Today is a good day for healing and evolution.

Exercise

In your present situation, ask yourself intuitively:

- *How old was I when this conflict began?*
- *Who was present with me when this occurred?*
- *What was it that occurred when this conflict began?*

Examine the needs that everyone in the situation was feeling.

- *What did you then decide about yourself, life, relationships, etc.?*

What you decided became your beliefs, and the world has recapitulated itself in terms of those beliefs. What you believe, you perceive. How you perceive comes from these beliefs and you act accordingly. This brings a response according to your belief and your belief is thus compounded and reinforced. Make new choices about what you want to believe now.

When you see yourself back at this conflict, imagine the light, the spirit in you, is reaching out and connecting with the light and spirit of everyone. This will bring peace and bonding. If it is a particularly strong trauma, you may need to repeat this joining of your light and theirs to build stronger and stronger bridges.

WAY 16 Sacrifice is a Form of Counterfeit Bonding

There is a spiritual form of sacrifice called 'a fire of sacrifice'. This week, choose to let go of an attachment for a lower order of thing. For example, let go of a desire of pornography, or a need to overdrink or overeat.

Sacrifice can be the letting-go of a lower form for something greater or more spiritual. When seen in its true light, this is not a loss. The sacrifice referred to in this book is an untrue form, a psychological mistake, or an attempt to make others lose or sacrifice even more than us.

Sacrifice is giving without receiving. In a spiritual sense, to give is to receive and to receive is to give. It is really give/receive. Giving allows us to connect or to realise the connections we have with those around us. Bonding is not something we do, it is something that *is*. It is a natural part of who we are with others, unless there is a conflict within which separates us from these others.

In psycho-dynamic terms, at the heart of any problem we find fear and separation. Healing either the fear or the separation effectively transforms the problem. Sacrifice is a mistaken solution to the need for inclusion. It sets up fusion, which is a confusion of personality boundaries in collusion with another.

Fusion is a counterfeit union or love. It comes from a position of sacrifice, built on guilt and trauma where we lost the realisation of bonding and began to sacrifice in an attempt to regain intimacy. Fusion is a counterfeit closeness that secretly thirsts for revenge.

Sacrifice can show itself in two ways. One is having to take care of someone else as an emotional or psychological burden. The other form of sacrifice is where we, as the more dependent person, give up our way of doing things to be taken care of by another. In the first form we believe we are a better, morally superior person, so it really does not matter if we have to carry someone or do it their way. In the second form of sacrifice we believe we are valueless so we attempt to be rid of ourselves, letting someone else carry us, letting their worth stand for both of us.

If we are in sacrifice with another person in any form, we have a solution that will not work. It is important not to compromise, as we will both feel that we have lost. Come to a resolution that is balanced, where both win. Sacrificing seeks closeness, but breeds resentment. Sacrifice is based on your guilt and only the innocence of everyone involved will allow a solution and a true bonding. Do not settle for less. Do not give up or adjust the situation. Want and choose the bonding. Choose everyone's innocence. Do not settle for sacrifice.

Sacrifice-fusion happens when we have lost our centre, which is a place of peace and grace. Our centre is the place where our higher mind works easily through us. This place that lacks bonding points to where bonding was lost through trauma in the womb or as a child. This was where we blamed ourselves for the troubles in our families and left our centres to try to do something about the problem. This place of lost bonding sets up separation and self-concepts to build our egos and at a certain point we begin to take on roles.

Over the years, my work has shown that figures can apply to the extent to which we have become uncentred. I found that if we got off our centre 1 to 30 percent, we have lived under an illusion, a misunderstanding, a mistake. If we got off our centre 30 to 80 percent, we have been in sacrifice. If we got off 80 to 99 percent, we have been in sacrifice to the point of self-destructiveness. If we got off our centre 100 percent, we killed that self, that central personality. The mind, prolific as it is, immediately gives us a new one. But we are already far off course. Our direction is skewed and our perception is faulty. We are in fusion, unsure of natural boundaries and as a result we may become needy in sacrifice or independent as a result of being in so much sacrifice.

Exercise

Today, ask your higher mind to carry you and those you dislike back to your centres. Ask your higher mind to carry everyone from the original event back to their centres. After you are carried back to your centre ask to be carried back to a higher centre if you are all not yet in a deep state of peace.

Feel the peace that comes to you as you reach your centre. What could take you months to attain (by going through traditional channels, such as psychotherapy, for example) would only take seconds if you allow your higher mind to do the work.

Ask to be carried back to progressively higher centres so there is finally a great deal of love and light.

WAY 17 Those We Dislike are Not Stopping Us from Receiving Love

Those we dislike are not stopping us from receiving love, we are. They are not stealing our partners' love from us. We only get the love we allow ourselves to receive. If someone seems to be intercepting the love coming to us, that is only how it seems on a conscious level. In truth we always receive love if we feel worthy of and are not afraid of it. We use others to people our conspiracy against ourselves.

Where someone else seems to have unnaturally heavy claims on our partners, there is a case of fusion going on. This is a blurring of the natural boundaries between two people. It is a form of sacrifice and hidden, or not-so-hidden, resentment. This speaks of an imbalance in our partners' family when they were growing up. But it could only be happening because there was also such an imbalance in our families, and we have a fusion going on. Our partner's fusion always makes us jealous or irritated to the extent that we have a fusion as well. This reflects a place where we are not yet committed to a partner because of that fusion. Every fusion is like a chain; while commitment in relationship brings us ease and paradoxically frees us, fusion belies truth and leads to heaviness, deadness and hard work.

A case of fusion suggests that there was a parent to whom we were very attached and a parent from whom we were more distant. The parent with whom we were more distant is typically the parent with whom we had problems. While the parent to whom we were attached is the parent with whom we have a bigger issue, we might feel much closer to them. We typically deal with our 'problem' parent first, and if we succeed, we move on to heal the issue with our fused parent. Fusion is a place of over-closeness or smothering. This does not necessarily take place behaviourally, but it always takes place emotionally or energetically. Sometimes in our teenage years we can have a reaction against the parent with whom we are fused in an attempt to find our own space or our own self. If we are fused with both parents then our partners are likely to become the 'outsiders' especially if they have different cultural roots.

Fusion is a form of sacrifice that does not allow us to receive or to succeed fully. Fusion is based on a guilt that secretly thirsts for revenge. It is the fusion-polarisation with our parents that is the root of patterns of over-closeness and distance with our parents-in-law or children. We must bring balance back to our minds and our families before we can be at peace in this whole area. It is these patterns in family dynamics that set up the negative relationship or victim patterns.

If we are in fusion with someone to that extent, our partners will be polarised from us. If we are polarised away from our partners, it is likely that they are in fusion with someone. Whatever it is, we are reliving early family experiences. This is the time when we can create a balance and a bonding with all concerned. We can have bonding and balance instead of blurred boundaries and sacrifice.

All family patterns are typically subconscious and are the root of our most chronic problems until we begin examining them.

Fusion is the root of co-dependency problems where one person is the enabler and the other is the identified problem person or addictive personality. Fusion is a place of counterfeit intimacy that does not allow receiving and generates an over-burdening sense of loyalty that we mistake for love. This mistake keeps us chained to people or situations and actually creates an 'enabling' situation rather than a helpful one. The enabling situation is where we are ostensibly the helper, but are secretly reinforcing the problem to keep ourselves needed. We do not actually want the other person to change or to get better and move forward because their movement would force us to do the same or be left behind. Our fear of moving forward is just as strong as that of the identified problem person.

Many times we may complain that a husband, wife, boyfriend or girlfriend is fused or overly attached to someone in their family. In this situation we will have a dislike and even a jealousy of them for interfering in our primary relationship. Yet this situation can only take place if we are also fused, even if it looks as though we are much more independent on the surface. Yet the more independent we are now, the more fused we once were – before

we burned out with sacrifice and became so independent. This may also show itself as old lovers,
friends, parents or even situations to which we are
fused. The amount of fusion is always equal with
partners though, ostensibly, one acts it out.

Exercise

*All of us have fusion, just as all of us have needs or polar-
isation (independence). Our commitment to ourselves, our
lives, our partners and healing our problems brings true
partnership, intimacy and success.*

*Close your eyes and feel or imagine being back with
your original family in the problem situation (character-
ised by fusion) that you have unearthed. This situation
will come to light when you examine your relationship
with your partner, and consider how you might react to
a relationship of theirs that seems to interfere or 'steal'
from your relationship.*

*Ask your higher mind to bring you back to your centre
in this situation. Ask that your higher mind bring your
whole family back to its centre in this situation and as
many centres as necessary to achieve a deep sense of light
and love in the scene.*

*Now ask that in your present situation you be brought
back to your centre, and that everyone in this situation
be carried back to their centres and every successive centre
necessary for true balance and bonding. You will know
when this is complete because you will feel peace, even
when thinking of those you dislike.*

WAY 18 Joining with Those We Dislike Will Create Healing

Our only real problem is separation, and seeing our interests as being different from others'. Dynamically this separation, which is synonymous with fear and attack thoughts, generates the proliferation of problems that we experience. When we feel separate, we act in a competitive way to further our interests, disregarding and objectifying those around us. Even winning the competition and having more than others naturally leads to alienation. The sense of separation becomes more pronounced when we either win or lose in a situation. Only co-operation and mutuality lead to joining and intimacy.

Fusion, which is a blurring of personal boundaries, is not joining. In fusion we feel in sacrifice and smothered, which leads us to run away or strike out in anger and attack in order to try and establish our differences. Joining at a conscious level is recognising that to give to another is to give to ourselves, just as to attack or judge another is to attack and punish ourselves. Joining is being in intimacy with a person where we 'dwell' with them, rather than turning them into an object to use, attack or blame.

When learning how to join, it is important that we learn to practise harmlessness. Harmlessness is a desire to bring no one harm. It is a way of being. Harmlessness creates another choice when we realise we are thinking thoughts that are not loving. Harmlessness is not subverted into other more hidden forms of attack, such as anxiety, pain, worry, concern, lust or so called 'constructive' criticism. Any thought without love and trust is an attack. Any thought is either loving or attacking, for there are no neutral thoughts. We turn a person into an object either by projecting negative feelings onto them (thus judging and attacking them), or projecting positive attributes onto them, but making them into an object to meet our needs.

Harmlessness knows that we reap what we sow, and that anything we do to others we do to ourselves. Joining is recognising that any true interest is a common interest. It recognises that whenever we compete to gain more than another we only find disappointment. Where we are seeking to gain more than another, whether it be beauty, intelligence, money or power, we will only find fleeting happiness. Competition will eventually lead to disillusionment and suffering.

Joining knows any fusion or any competition is actually a way to avoid taking the next step. Both are ways we seek to take from another. This delays us and has us looking in the wrong direction for our happiness. We then fall into the biggest mistake of assigning to others a secondary place in the 'movie' of our lives as we play the 'heroes' or 'stars', making others merely objects to meet our needs. This will lead to upset if they do not accept the script we assigned to them, or boredom, and the eventual sacrifice of having to 'carry' them.

On the other hand, joining really moves us forward. By joining with another, we are both brought to a new level of intimacy and a new level of confidence. A common weal that springs up in intimacy gives one a feel of common goal, a common humanity and shared family. It is the beginning of the experience that all of us are here for each other. When things are their highest and best we seem to know that. Joining gives us the feeling of winning together that provides both the love and the joy that come from connectedness.

Exercise

Imagine that someone you dislike is across from you in a large room. The distance between you is in reality the separateness and judgement between you. Imagine that each step towards that person is a step in healing that distance. Take step after step towards them in your mind's eye as you feel willing to bridge the gap between you. If you feel resistance, feel the discomfort until it is gone and ask your higher mind for help.

As you finally reach that person, look into their eyes and see the child inside them that wants your love, implores your love, invites your love. Reach out and take their hands. Hear their call for help, their call to be saved, their call to save you. Imagine now that who is before you is a part of yourself you have judged, fragmented and repressed, and you have finally come to redeem yourself, to forgive yourself. Integrate the lost part of you that has been causing an invisible barrier in your forward movement.

WAY 19 Those We Dislike are Not Traps

Those we dislike are not traps unless we make them into traps. A trap is a problem person or situation that or who causes us to become stuck rather than moving forward. We obsess about traps, and they are an obstruction to peace. It is peace from which joy, love and movement forward are generated.

Any situation, no matter how dire, need not be used as an obstacle to peace. It is through peace that all things unfold graciously and naturally. Any extreme situation is also a situation that can be used to springboard us forward to a new level of consciousness, and to heal that which is fractured within us. It is a test or an invitation to a new level of being . . . one we can take willingly or one we can be dragged through. It is up to us.

We can use traps to stop ourselves from moving forward because we are frightened of the next step. A trap can be used to block a gift, opportunity or talent because we are afraid of the level of surrender these benefits call for within us. A trap is built on guilt, some kind of bad feeling that keeps us withdrawn and out of the flow of life. A trap keeps us self-conscious when others most need our help. It keeps us self-centred and even selfishly indulgent when it is most important that we extend ourselves both for ourselves and others.

A trap is a form of delay that builds on the separation in the world and reinforces belief in suffering, destruction and death. Moving through our traps and limitations is the best thing we can do to help the world to evolve. Every step we take forward both inspires and teaches others that they can do the same, and allows a grace to heal others. It gives both permission and supports others to do the same. There is a good chance we will not get through all of the limitations surrounding us, but each one we do get past helps to clear the minefield for those who come after us. It is most helpful for our children.

One of the basic ways to move out of a trap is first to realise that we are in one. A trap is a problem for which we are afraid to find the solution because it is asking us to change in some way. Whenever a problem emerges, a solution emerges at the same time. If we have the courage to accept that solution, everything prospers. Finding the solution immediately means that we avoid abusing time, for if we waste time, time wastes us. Once we realise we are in a trap we can use our most powerful tool, the power of choice. We can choose not to be trapped.

Exercise

In any situation in your life where there is a trap, use these statements to move out of your obsession and into peace. Use these powerful words to help move you forward. They will remove the trap, or at least a major layer of it.

*Use them as many times as necessary. Fill the words with
your energy, your will and the power of your choice.*

*'I will not use this as a trap. I will not use this to hold
me back. But I will use it as a means to truth, peace and
leaping forward.'*

Understanding Opens the
Door to Forgiveness and
Appreciation Opens the
Door to Love

There is, in truth, nothing that needs to be forgiven
by anyone. When we reach forgiveness, we realise this.
Given inner and outer pressures, we do the best we
can, yet we are all able to do better. We make mistakes. We get caught in traps and chronic patterns,
striving to win at our particular life game or way of
seeing the world, without realising that we are called
for something much greater. In order to free ourselves
to answer this call we must change our ways of living
or our perceptions of the world.

The fact that we have someone in our world who
is caught in a trap (and is seemingly infringing on us)
is not accidental. At a subconscious level there is collusion. If we look, we will find a hidden conflict in
us calling for healing, and an opportunity to learn
something that would advance and strengthen us. It
is our forgiveness that allows this to be accomplished.
It is an opportunity for us to become increasingly
harmless and innocent.

Through our aggression, attacking thoughts and
victimisation (another form of attack), we have probably noticed that we are not completely harmless.
We may even have noticed that our sacrifice in this

situation is actually a manipulation to force others to lose the game and to sacrifice more than us in order that we may get our own way. Those who are whole make no demands.

We are not in any particular situation by accident, but by design. We can do much to further ourselves and others by becoming willing to understand all of the levels of what is taking place. Once someone understands, they feel no need to forgive, realising that there has simply been a mistake. Through these circumstances, life is telling us about an aspect within ourselves that can be resolved. If we refuse the lesson, it will typically become a trial for us. Here is a chance to learn of our wholeness, which this conflict is obscuring from us.

Giving our appreciation is another possible way of moving through a conflict (or one layer of the conflict at a time). Appreciation sets up a flow, whereas judgement and grievance lock us into the situation. The appreciation may only be at the level of discovering we have finally identified this conflict inside us which has been eating away at us without our awareness, and stealing energy to keep the conflict locked away. In other words, while we may not appreciate a person, or a relationship, we can appreciate that they brought to our attention a conflict or grievance that we may not have known was there.

If we can appreciate that a conflict has brought to light something to heal instead of allowing it to leech our energy, then this in itself is a beginning. Notice how much of this book has centred on motivating us to change and deal with situations in a new light. Motivation creates change.

Exercise

Imagine how the person with whom you're not getting along must be feeling to act in the way they are acting. Have you ever been in a position to experience this feeling? Remember what you were going through when you felt this way, and how it affected you. Knowing this feeling so well yourself, can you understand what this person is going through? It is probably a remnant of this old feeling inside you that is causing the conflict. Now is the opportunity to release yourself by not holding it against them.

Imagine that you are someone you dislike. Imagine what it is like waking up in the morning as them . . . how things feel, what the world looks like to them, how their day goes, what they are thinking about, where they feel threatened. Imagine all of their interactions and feelings until they go to bed at night. Take at least ten minutes for this exercise.

List in your mind or on paper all of the things you really appreciate about that person. Any good qualities they have, any kindnesses they may have done for you or your family, or any support they may have given are likely areas to explore. Dwell on these things, or on just one of these things if it stands out for you. This appreciation will move you forward.

Since awareness of your wholeness would free you, concentrate on this today by blessing the person with whom you're not getting along. For example, you might repeat the following statement with them in mind today, or use the name of anyone else who seems to be giving you trouble, or anyone who comes to mind, saying:

'My wholeness blesses you,_____ (name).'

Repeat this throughout the day.

WAY 21 Our Balance Helps More Than Just Ourselves

Balance is a state of mind where peace resides. It is unruffled by the ups and downs of fortune. It is neither passive nor static, but responsive and connected. It gives and receives. While not relying on itself, balance has both the courage to lead and the intelligence to allow group strength and the higher mind to achieve success rather than simply cope with the status quo.

Our balance and evenness are a benefit to our partners and families, as they can rely on this steadiness rather than the vagaries of emotion and mood. When reactive or aggressive energy comes our way, balance calmly recognises attack as a call for help, a chance to grow and strengthen and an opportunity for new learning and greater contact.

Emotions have a way of triggering each other. This is obvious in cases of fear or anger. A person who is willing not to buy into a reactive emotional situation is the person who can change or begin to change the pattern. This person, by their balance and vision, can close the door to hysteria and the attack of reactive emotion.

Every family has a group-mind which is constantly seeking to balance itself through the actions of its members. One person striving for truth and a responsive balance, rather than always feeding the family drama, can do much to unfold a family towards its purpose.

Another way to understand our families is to see each member as a representation of a subconscious part of our minds. These parts are actually fractured and repressed parts of us. As we find the parts of our own minds that each member of our family represents, and integrate these aspects, we will see a corresponding change in the family members. In a similar way our friends, acquaintances, work associates and even people we see and read about represent parts of our own minds.

Our interactions with these people are a measure of the interaction in our own minds, with the selves with whom we identify, and other less identified personalities that are projected onto others in our world. In one sense the world as we see it is within our minds, and one person truly dedicated can do much good in the world just by changing their mind, and increasing their balance. It is this balance that allows both inspiration and grace to come through to right the situation. It is the maturity of balance that allows both for truth and valuing only that which is truly valuable.

The whole world is inextricably interconnected. An act of kindness, generosity or love adds to the light of the whole world. What we do with those around us with whom we are interconnected can bless the entire world.

A single heartfelt giving could allow a mother on the other side of the planet to find food for her starving child. One act of forgiveness could allow a would-be suicide half the world away to pull the gun from his head and make another choice. A loving gesture, a spontaneous, heartfelt response could allow a spring to rise up in the desert.

Conversely, the wars of the world, its famines and plagues reflect deep unconscious patterns in us all. Yet one person truly dedicated to humanity and service could provide a healing that would create a corresponding effect in the world. Truly, we are the world and its people. Our balance aids our own evolution and assists the evolution of the planet.

Exercise

Here is an integration exercise that can take away any conflict and join you at least one layer closer to those around you – for example, your family. It will also take you one step and one layer closer to life. You can do this more often if you have chronic problems.

Imagine the family you grew up with standing around you in a circle. Know they are reflections of your own mind. As aspects of your mind, invite them to come to you one by one, joining you and melting into you.

Next imagine any people with whom you are having problems and then once again have each of them stand in a circle, come up to you, melt into you and integrate with you.

Spend a few minutes thinking of all of the calls for help in the world today. If it is useful, think of everything in the world that is not love. These things are a call for help. If you are willing to help it becomes easy to hear all of the cries for help. Today, be aware of all those with whom you come in contact, knowing that no meeting is by chance. Use this day to make a difference to them, to the world and to yourself.

Do not use these calls for help as a means to avoid your purpose because this is the best way to help the world – and yourself. You can respond with a lovingness and a blessing. Your responsiveness will create a flow, whereas avoidance and over-inclusiveness (an overburdening sense of loyalty) would simply be a trap to distract and slow yourself down. Your discernment and balance will show you the difference.

An Attack on Somone We
Dislike is Really an Attack
on Our Partners

Any attack on another is actually an attack meant for
our partners or the ones closest to us. It is much
easier to displace upset onto someone seemingly outside our relationships, than to be aware and deal with
the aspects that are incomplete and troubling us in
our relationships. This way of looking at our grievances with others is a way to bring that which is subconscious into our consciousness so we can deal with
it.

Furthermore, what we hold against any one person,
we actually hold against everyone, including our partners. If our mate was doing what we are upset at
others for doing, we would be holding it against our
mate. And we actually are, because the distance we
keep from one person actually keeps a wedge between
us and everyone. In other words, any conflict that we
have outside our relationships actually reflects conflict within our closest relationships.

Forgiving something in anyone is to forgive it in
everyone, including ourselves. To forgive an issue is
to transform our perception of it so we either no
longer perceive it as being a problem or we perceive
it as a call for help to which we can easily respond.
Either way, forgiveness leads to peace.

It takes a natural intuitiveness, or a good level of communication, to ferret out the hidden issues between us and our partners, but it is truly worth doing. This is because the hidden issue is affecting us even though we are not aware of it. Awareness of a problem is half the battle. It is also important to be aware of the fact that as soon as a problem appears, so does the answer. While our actual experiences may differ from this, it is important to know that the principle is true and that our answers will appear as soon as we are truly ready to accept them. The amount of time it takes for us to get an answer is the amount of time it takes for us to have confidence about the next step, the next level of success.

Some deep, fertile and productive communication between us and our partners can occur when we choose a someone that our partners or we ourselves are not getting along with, and then begin to explore the hidden or not so hidden issues in our relationships these might implicate. But it is important to do so with the goal of moving our relationships closer. We can create a bridge of bonding where previously there was only conflict.

If we begin to explore the concept of this lesson by reflecting on our relationships in a light fashion, and with a positive attitude, we can really 'make a difference'. For example, let's suppose there is something to this concept, and let's talk about this conflict with a person with whom we are not getting along as if it really was a hidden conflict in our own relationship with a partner. What do we have to lose by examining this? Our relationships can only get better if we work together to realise a new bonding.

This principle can begin to make conscious all that is subconscious in our relationship. What we bring from the darkness into the light can be more easily healed. It is also important to remember that a hidden interpersonal conflict between ourselves and our partners is really an intra-psychic conflict, a conflict within each of us individually. It is the responsibility of both our partners and ourselves, and in that way we can heal it together. This especially applies to a person who is closest to us – a child, a parent, a lover or a friend.

Using this method can actually create not only shifts in our relationships, but corresponding shifts in the person with whom we are not getting along.

Exercise

If you have someone close to you with whom you can communicate in this fashion, use this principle to explore your relationship. This can be some of the most exciting and fruitful communication you can have. When you have the attitude that there are no 'bad guys' in your relationship, and what you are working towards is innocence and freedom for both of you together as a team, you have penetrated to a level that generates interdependence in your relationship, and inspiration and leadership to others.

If you do not have someone with whom to explore this level of relationship, then take some quiet time by yourself. Ask the help of your higher self. Clear your mind of any extraneous thoughts, and be open to impressions, intuitions and thoughts that come to you in this regard. See how these thoughts fit a pattern you have experienced before.

Conjure up the negative feelings you have towards someone you dislike. Examine whether you have experienced the feelings you are now experiencing before. With whom did you experience these feelings and in what regard? Does this mean a pattern of feelings have existed at least since childhood? As you become aware of this pattern ask your higher mind to clear it for you. When you take full responsibility for an experience in your life, you can then ask your higher mind to clear it for you.

Imagine that the block between you and another is responsible for a certain amount of distance between you and the person closest to you. Now imagine that your partner is with you in a certain room and put them across the room from you. Focusing on the issue with the other person, ask yourself what is holding you back from them. As you acknowledge what it is, ask yourself if you're willing to let it go. If you are, take a step forward. Now ask what's holding you back from your partner. As you recognise this and are willing to let it go, step forward. Do this same thing until you can work your way across to your partner and embrace them . . . If your partner is willing, you can do this together, taking alternate turns.

As an alternative, you can dialogue with your partner about the issue with the other as showing a place where you haven't come together. Do this until you feel joined fully with your partner.

WAY 23 On Both Sides of a Conflict People are Acting in Opposite Ways and Feeling the Same Thing

In any conflict people may be acting in completely opposite fashions, such as victimiser-victim, fight-flight or hysterical-stoical. Yet both parties are feeling exactly the same emotion, even if they are not consciously aware of it. For instance, there is as much anger or violence in a victim as there is in a victimiser, and fear generates both fight and flight. In any conflict we feel as if our position is correct and we fight for being right. Yet if we recognised that we are actually feeling the same thing that our opponent is feeling, it can become a point of sharing, mutual identification and even the beginning of agreement.

The first step is to recognise what it is we are feeling, remembering that feelings such as anger actually hide deeper emotions, such as hurt, fear or guilt. We may be acting in a dissociated manner to avoid feeling the pain, but our defensiveness belies the pain. As we get in touch with the feelings we are experiencing, we have the basis for understanding what the other person is feeling and, thus, why they are acting as they are. We also have the basis for communication because we have a mutual point of contact.

The second step is to invite them into communication where this is possible. For example: 'Are you feeling afraid?' or 'I have been feeling guilty for some reason, and it has interfered with our relationship. Have you been feeling negative feelings, too?' Many times it is more successful if we share our feelings and check to see if they are feeling similarly.

This is the first point of joining, and a place where our understanding can begin to give us confidence. It can also be the beginning of uncovering the self-deception that is present on both sides in any conflict.

Exercise

Today, get in touch with what it is you are feeling and experiencing in a conflict. Begin communication around this experience, looking for a place of mutuality. When this is found, neither of you will look at the other as the enemy. Communication is the beginning of forgiveness. You can even realise partnership by moving through this experience together in communication.

Expectations are Hidden
Demands

Whenever we find ourselves frustrated or disappointed, it is because we have an expectation of someone or something. We judge that something should be different than it is. This type of response is an expectation, and it creates stress. An expectation is some form of 'should', 'have to', 'need to', 'ought to' or 'must'. It is a demand on ourselves or on others.

When demands are placed upon someone to do something under duress (a form of sacrifice that does not allow them to receive), most people will acquiesce. Or they will not do what is demanded of them because they feel pressured. The same thing occurs when we make demands on ourselves.

To ask, invite or inspire others opens up the flow of life, rather than trying to push or force it. Expectations block communications because they are a form of force which demands that others change and meet our needs. This creates resistance and power struggle and stops forward progress.

Demands come out of our needs; wholeness would make no demands. We demand of others that which we are not doing ourselves. For instance, if we expect someone to love us, it is because we are not loving ourselves or even them for that matter, confusing our needs with love. When we demand rather than choose or prefer, we push people away from us. Demanding that our needs are met by others demonstrates a conflict within ourselves. Even if we get what we have demanded, it will not satisfy or empower us. Only that which we give/receive can do that.

Expectations hide attachments, and it is the holding-on that prevents our receiving. All attachments are forms of demands on life. When we have them, we are not successful and our lives do not unfold. Sooner or later, this is why what we become attached to, what we think of as the source of our happiness, is lost to us. Yet in our loss and disillusionment there is the hope of moving forward.

An expectation is hidden pain that will surface sooner or later, bringing its burden with it. This is why letting go of attachments allows us to move forward easily. Letting go is merely the recognition that an illusion cannot make us happy. To let go is not to throw away, but merely to place things in their proper perspective and in their right relationships. Anything else is an illusion, and when we spend a great deal of time and energy investing in an illusion, we are sure to be disillusioned.

Wherever there is a conflict there are expectations and demands. As we become aware of these expectations, we realise that they will keep a conflict going. Conversely, letting go of our expectations can move the conflict on to the next level which needs to be healed (the next level of expectations) or it can resolve it altogether.

The first of the two most common forms of letting

go of attachment is finding the need or pain underneath and feeling it until it is completely dissipated.
The second is just giving our need or pain or attachment into the hands of our higher mind.

Exercise

*Examine the 'shoulds' and 'need to's' you have in relation
to others. Examine all of the 'shoulds' and 'need to's' you
have in this conflict with the person with whom you are
not getting along. You may find it helps to ask yourself
questions over and over again to see what intuitively comes
up. You might ask such questions as:*

> *This person should* _____
> *This person needs to* _____
> *I should* _____
> *In this situation my partner should* _____

*Another way to do this is to examine areas where you
have an upset or judgement, because these are areas where
there are hidden demands and needs.*

*Through 'burning' away the feelings underneath, or
turning these feelings or attachments over to your higher
mind, begin the letting-go process.*

*Your willingness to forgive your needs/expectations and
to forgive the other person's needs/fears/demands can serve
to release you both.*

*Your willingness to say yes to the next step (visualise
and allow the next step to come to you) would also cut
through both your own demands, and those of the person*

with whom you are not getting along, thereby freeing your-
self to move to the next level.

   Now let go of these attitudes, turning them over to your
higher mind.

WAY 25 Guilt is Merely a Trap

As human beings we feel guilty about a myriad of things. Virtually all the bad feelings we have, such as sadness, hurt, sacrifice, needs and fear, also carry an adjunctive feeling of guilt. Guilt keeps us living in the past rather than in the present moment. Guilt does not see mistakes that need correction; it sees badness that deserves and needs punishment.

Guilt is such a painful feeling, we typically project it out and see others as worthy of punishment. Guilt easily hides under judgements and grievances.

Guilt is not helpful in any way. It does not assist change, but keeps us stuck in a trap. It is the 'super glue' of life. Guilt throws us into unworthiness and sacrifice, feelings of failure and deadness, valuelessness and lack of commitment. Guilt becomes self-destructive, and creates emotional fusion; it builds a monument to a mistake at which we worship. It takes a mistake and obsesses about it rather than using it as a means to learn a lesson and move forwards. It cuts us off from inspiration, intuition and vision. It is a personal ecological disaster based on a form of arrogance and dark glamour. It puts us at the centre of things and it either turns all the attention on us or we seek to withdraw or disappear. Guilt is linked to some form of attack, either overt or through withdrawal, which is just as violent a form of aggression in its own way as active attack.

The bottom line is that guilt hides fear because when we are guilty, we are afraid to face the next step. All of us have loads of guilt, but guilt is untrue and it keeps us from repenting, learning the lesson and correcting the mistake. Guilt invests itself in separateness as the guilty are ever alone in their guilt.

With someone we dislike there is inevitably guilt or bad feeling, and we have used this as a trap. Refuse to allow this to continue. It is important to not use it on ourselves or others, or to allow them to use it on us. Guilt will hide the truth in the situation. The truth will allow us to respond in such a way as to move things forward. Be willing to get back on the path of life and take the next step. Let no vestige of guilt that hides in grievance or judgement hinder our evolution. Let no areas where we are working hard, but making no progress, hide guilt and hamper us. Let none of the overcompensations of sacrifice and untrue giving hide guilt. Let no demand or attack camouflage it.

If we are not harmless, we are projecting our guilt and attacking it outside ourselves in others to cover how we actually think about ourselves. Guilt is one of the most destructive forces in our world. The punishment we mete out to ourselves is never enough, because even punishment makes us feel bad and guilty, and this guilt reinforces the very things about which we feel guilty in the first place. It gives all the attention to the mistake, the problem and ourselves, rather than to the solution.

Exercise

Today, focus on areas of guilt, sacrifice and grievances, paying particular attention to situations with those you dislike. If you find any areas about which you feel bad, then choose not to use this as a trap, but to move forward to give/receive in life again. Be willing to learn any lessons or to correct any mistakes as you do so. You can do this through the power of choice.

Examine any form of sacrifice or fusion as a place where guilt hides. Ask your higher mind to release you from the self-centredness of guilt that keeps you off your true centre. Ask for your higher mind to move you back into your centre so you might know the truth. Your centre is a place of peace and innocence.

Be willing to release your grievances and the guilt hiding underneath them in order to move forward. Choose to let these grievances go to improve your life and your relationships. As you let grievances towards others go it removes the subconscious guilt that both keeps you feeling bad and generates painful experiences to pay off guilt.

WAY 26 Acceptance Heals Conflicts

Wherever there is a conflict there is something we will not accept. Our rejection or resistance actually creates the feeling of hurt or rejection and, of course, 'what you resist persists'. Our resistance keeps the conflict from changing or unfolding. We are locked into the very thing we abhor until, paradoxically, we accept it. When we stop trying to change someone and either accept them as they are or actually do what is true for us, the person or situation changes.

Conflict is a fight for the positions of dominance and sacrifice. Even when we are in sacrifice ourselves, we are attempting to force someone else to sacrifice more than we are.

As we accept, we allow the situation to progress, unfold and evolve to the next step. Yet many of us are afraid that if we accept the situation, it will continue unabated. But it is only our resistance and sacrifice that allows a painful situation to continue. Sacrifice is a form of losing in a conflict in order to be the 'morally superior' person, or to lose now so that others might lose more in the long run. On the other hand, acceptance allows the outer situation to unfold as we integrate the inner fragmented parts of our minds that helped to create the conflict on the outside.

As an example, let's take a scenario that many

people fear – that of a personal tragedy. If we don't accept it, the pain of the tragedy remains with us, ever alive and never far from awareness. But if we accept what has occurred, we are able to leap forward in consciousness and awareness. In fact, the bigger the tragedy, the more you leap forward on the path of life. Many of these tragic events are actually initiations, recapitulations or shamanic tests that have the power either to kill you or to make you wise. Acceptance allows you to pass the test. What is accepted is integrated, so the lesson is no longer necessary. Conversely, we never accept in others what we actually believe, but do not accept about ourselves.

Since conflict comes out of self-deception, we usually don't recognise conflict until it is upon us. This self-deception usually leads to self-righteousness in the situation, because we don't realise our parts in it. The conflict is actually an opportunity for the healing of hidden elements within us, and growth in areas where we seemed invisible (as in the case of the person with whom we are not getting along).

Our grievance in this situation keeps us frightened, because when we attack, we expect to be attacked back. We could be totally safe if we gave up all of our grievances. It is harmlessness that opens the door of grace; harmlessness that allows us to give and receive freely. It is harmlessness that furthers all true evolution and allows us to be aware of the interconnectedness of all things.

Our grievances in a situation block inspiration and our higher minds. The noise of our attack and righteousness does not allow the intuitive answer that would resolve things for everyone, not only now, but forever. The power of our higher mind to heal and find solutions is blocked by our pain. Pain will show up as resistance, emotional blackmail and sacrifice, which is a way of losing now to win later. This attempt at winning through competition leads us to close off the higher mind and to rely on ourselves to win. To utilise the higher mind is to find the answer to any problem as soon as we are ready to hear it.

Acceptance also allows us to receive, whereas conflict blocks receiving. Our acceptance of the situation allows us to accept the healing, the gifts and the grace that are being offered in this situation.

Exercise

Today, think of someone you dislike, and look for some element to which you are attached and haven't been willing to let go. Look for what it is you refuse to accept and would rather fight about. Acknowledge what it is you could lose by not accepting this (for example, being beyond this situation, having the wisdom and power to successfully graduate from this situation, losing contact with your higher mind and its ability to find a solution where you both win in seemingly impossible situations, release from fear in situations like this, etc.).

Make another choice about what you want now.

Go back through your life, looking for situations that still hurt or feel bad. Once again, go through the steps of the exercise, write down what it was you lost and what it might be possible to gain now as a result of finally accepting

the situation. Do this until you can accept these situations
and feel energised and empowered by them.

For any situations you feel you can't accept, ask the
help of your higher mind.

Our conflict distracts us from our personal purpose and evolution. Personal service and world evolution become ancillary to us during the drama of a conflict. Many times we create the conflict because we are afraid of our personal purpose and so seek to distract ourselves away from it.

Distractions and traps abound. They pull our attention away from what is really important and what really adds to our happiness. This conflict is such a distraction. It closes off inspiration and intuition which would show us the way through the conflict. It has us emphasise righteousness and domination instead of truth. In the pain and obsession of the fight, we miss the simple joys and the importance of our mates, children, families, communities and our spiritual-psychological growth.

Our purpose is never more than we can handle, though the thought of it is sometimes both thrilling and frightening. Our purpose does not specifically comprise things we do, though this may be part of it. It is something we are; an aspect of our being that radiates out to the world. Fear of purpose is the underlying cause of the vast majority of conflicts, problems, traps and distractions. Because we are afraid that we are not 'big' or confident enough to make a difference or to accomplish our purpose, we create traumatic or problematic situations to block what is truly important and living our purpose.

Our purpose is about happiness. If we are not happy, our purpose begins with forgiveness, harmlessness, healing and service, so happiness can be achieved. In addition to happiness, our personal purpose has to do with that focus or function that only we can fulfil. All of these aspects lead to happiness and fulfilment. To change our conflicts into something that adds to personal and world purpose would require dedicating ourselves to harmlessness and healing the problem.

Most personal problems fall away when someone dedicates themselves to their personal purpose and the service it generates. This is because many problems just serve as a conspiracy against having to live our purpose. Yet it is our purpose that leads ultimately to our fulfilment. Our closest relationships are vital to the fulfilment of our purpose. They provide meaning and energy for our lives. What has true meaning is life enhancing, has youthening effects, and has encouragement for our personal evolution as well as world evolution. Yet this purpose may be as simple and profound as loving everyone we come in contact with as much as we can.

Living one's purpose
is leaping the abyss to love,
    and leaving a bridge
        for others to follow.

Chuck Spezzano, *Awaken the Gods*

Living our purpose allows for a visionary state of being. This is a level of love and creativity that provides a positive future, an expanded awareness and an excitement about life and other people.

Most people shy away from their purpose for fear they will have to do it, or fear of losing something to which they are attached. But vision is not something we do, it is something done through us. In vision there is a sense of life living us, rather than us living life. It feels like we are our best selves.

Furthermore, whatever it is that we are afraid to let go, which keeps us from our purpose, is an attachment that must be given up if life is to unfold and progress. When we have an attachment or a need, we try to get or take rather than receive. It blocks our ability to be self-confident, trusting, open and receptive. It counterfeits possessiveness for love. What we hold onto can never make us happy; it dooms us to shattered dreams and disillusionment. What we seek in attachment can only be found in living our purpose.

Living your purpose is keeping the promise made before you came to earth. It is your fulfilment.

Exercise

Decide today that you will not use a person with whom you're not getting along to hold you back or distract you from your purpose. Ask your higher mind to show you your life purpose, or at least the next step in your life purpose. See your forgiveness of this conflict as fitting your purpose. Be willing to be a world server if only by raising your own consciousness. As you step forward, transcending limitations and opening to a new level, grace can pour into you and others in similar situations around the world. As you live your purpose, you begin to catch glimpses of the world plan or purpose that is unfolding and evolving along with you.

Most of the problems and traumas in your life have been there to hide your life purpose, yet the resolution of these problems and patterns helps to unveil and fulfil it. Choose not to let this most precious gift and means of fulfilment be hidden from you any longer. Choose to know yourself and your gift to life. Choose to know how you fit into the unfolding world plan and purpose.

Those We Dislike Have
Come to Save Us

Today, we shall take a look at a more advanced concept, which approaches our conflict from a new perspective. As we change our perspective, our perception changes, and so the situation itself changes. At some level, all healing is a change in the way we see things.

The situation between us and whomever we have been in dispute has been shifting level by level. This process occurs because many of our conflicts are multi-levelled, and sometimes we are angry or are in conflict about a number of different things. This is also why this is a fifty-way book. It allows the most chronic conflicts to be moved through layer by layer. While any one of the lessons could resolve the conflict, fifty ways provides the means (given any kind of willingness) to move through the layers of the most intricate conflicts.

To change our perspectives, we will need to be willing to give up being right. We cannot be right and have healing too. Our change of perspective is the basis of our successful resolution of this situation. This takes the readiness to be a willing learner – even a happy learner!

Our righteousness states there is nothing more we can learn, the case is closed and we have the answer already. The problem with righteousness is that when we decided we were right about how things are, we became stuck with the situation, exactly as it is. But if we are willing to be mistaken, there are all kinds of possibilities that might unfold.

Today's new perspective comes from seeing those we dislike as being responsible for saving us. They have come to save us, giving us an opportunity to clear out a conflict within us, which has been eating away at us, using up inner resources and stopping our forward progress with an invisible wall that has thwarted our best efforts to move beyond it. Now the conflict within us is out in the open. If we resist the illusion that this is just someone else's problem or fault, we can be blessed with the awareness that we do have a problem and what the nature of it is. We can be shown discernment as to what and how much is ours to heal and how much to let go. This is half the battle, and we will know what needs work.

Again, any attempts to change someone with whom we're not getting along, through active or aggressive means, is in fact a denial of our own responsibility, and it prevents us from being able to change the situation. Any attempt to punish them by withdrawal or emotional blackmail of negative emotion, again confuses the issue and affects our ability to transform the situation. Any attempts to manipulate the situation causes us to lose this golden opportunity. Remaining harmless in the face of this attack or problem leads to an evolution in maturity. Even if the person with whom we're not getting along is the most evil person on the planet, by choosing not to be a victim and quite possibly not remaining in relationship with such a person, we can still greatly evolve through harmlessness and forgiveness. Instead of becoming upset or angry when we think of them, we can choose to send them a blessing, or love or light, which evolves us quickly and successfully to a position where we can help both the person in question, and the planet as a whole.

Another major benefit that results from a situation surrounding someone with whom we are not getting along, is that it focuses our guilt through 'their' problem. In other words, what would be elusively subconscious is now made evident. Again, only the guilty condemn, and only the self-accused accuse others. But here, by our forgiveness, we offer them help rather than condemn them. By offering them help we release them from our projection and quite possibly others' projections as well. We also release ourselves. As we save them from this conflict with our forgiveness and harmlessness, they can then give us a level of support we had not anticipated. As we save them they can come full circle and save us. With each grievance forgiven, the person with whom we're not getting along can become more and more beautiful. There is only beauty where there is forgiveness and love. Again, as we forgive someone, our perception and our experience of them changes. As we release our guilt, we see them more clearly and they respond to that clarity and lack of projection.

Let us again exaggerate to make a point and take a 'fantastic,' worse-case scenario. Let us say that the person with whom we're not getting along was the devil incarnate, sent from hell especially to give us a bad time. Forgiveness and harmlessness would neutralise them, render the evil incapable of harming us and set them on a path of evolution that they might hate at first, but later appreciate. Continued forgiveness would continue the transformation. Evil has access to us only through our own negative thoughts or attacks.

The resolution of conflicts releases stress, gives us increased mercy, improves our health, frees us to move forward, allows us to receive more without effort, promotes a greater sense of well-being and creates greater clarity, confidence and intimacy. It can lessen fear and give us a greater sense of innocence. This is not a complete list, but one which can give us an idea of the benefits of a healing resolution to conflict.

Exercise

Today, recognise your ability to choose to see conflict situations differently and to commit to the transformation of your perception (which is your projection). Commit to the release of yourself and the others involved from the little piece of hell that every conflict contains.

Realise that your grievance is just your belief that you know what is going on and what is right in the situation. To presume to know this on all levels of process and unfolding is certainly arrogant. But it is your forgiveness and harmlessness that puts things in their proper perspective and allows you to see clearly. Choice, commitment and attitude, choosing and then rechoosing are all it takes to make change.

Choose to free yourself and the others through

harmlessness and forgiveness. If this does not happen easily, call in your higher mind to accomplish it for you.

WAY 29 Judging Judgement

Judgement, which leads to grievances, stops forward progression, development and the natural unfolding of a happy life. Once we have judged someone, they stop growing. We have made up our mind, the case is closed, and all we need is for the sentence to be carried out because the verdict has been delivered: guilty as charged, deserving of punishment. It is crucial to remember that we will not escape the judgement and the punishment we make on others.

Judgement is inherently dishonest because it is based on our guilt. In other words, we only judge if we feel bad about something in ourselves. When we judge, we never see the whole picture so it is never correct. We are basically only judging our own self-concepts and our own negative beliefs within ourselves as we try to perceive the world through them.

Judgement stops inspiration, grace and our higher mind. We have already picked a scapegoat, and denied our own responsibility. The more we judge, the worse we feel. This is easily evidenced by being aware of how we feel as we judge someone, or some situation.

All we need to do is think of someone we are judging and notice how we are feeling as we judge them. If we notice what is happening with our energy, we notice that the judgements we make are literally exhausting us.

We compensate for our guilt by making ideals. We then judge anyone who does not live up to them. Some people are so caught in this early stage of development that they make their religion or political beliefs into the compensation that will save them. This is a level that the more extreme forms of fundamentalism and communism are caught in. Then they see everyone not living by their beliefs as worthy of death or hell.

To get along with someone we must give up our judgements. Otherwise, we will punish them for what we feel guilty about. If we do not judge them, we will perceive any negative behaviour as just a call for help and respond to this call. If we let go of our judgement, if we help, we release our own mistaken guilt with which we have been attacking ourselves. As we let go of our judgements on others, they grow and unfold to become better. Otherwise, our judgement is constantly reinforcing another's mistakes. The world is our mirror. At one level we are only pointing the finger of judgement at ourselves.

Without judgement, there would be no separation but a natural friendship, connection and bonding with another. This relationship, based on co-operation, would be synergistic, abundant and happy, whether it is with an acquaintance, a colleague or family member.

If all the judgement in us were gone, the light within us would shine out. We would be enlightened, and know ourselves as the pure love and will of our spirit. We would see ourselves as part of *All That Is* and we would experience the ecstasy of union and Oneness.

We think we would be helpless without the judgement of our egos but it is like a rose protecting itself with its little thorns. Our ego has its own agenda and uses investments, such as fear, guilt and competition to keep separation and its own self-identity going. The judgements of the ego lead to self-attack and death. On the other hand, we could let the judgement and discernment of our higher mind make the necessary choices and changes that would have a situation move forward where everyone could succeed without anyone having to sacrifice. When the ego judges, someone has to sacrifice. When we judge someone and decide they are wrong or bad, we immediately feel victimised by them. It is only our own judgements that put us into sacrifice.

Exercise

Today, commit to giving up judgement.

First of all, recognise that those you have been judging need your help. Your judgement makes you feel in sacrifice. Your blessing them would bless both of you. Your responding to their need would free you both.

Second, take the one person who seems to be really bothering you. You have probably been thinking of that person already. Take a quiet moment and ask yourself: 'What is it they need?' For example, if you have a friend who is starting to annoy you, and you ask yourself 'what is it that they need', you'll probably find words such as love, support, encouragement, attention, understanding or forgiveness popping into your mind. Now imagine that whatever came to your mind was given to them by you – not only on a surface level, but energetically to their hearts and minds.

Do this on as many levels as possible. It will free you both. When you learn to meet the perceived needs in people rather than judging them, there is no situation that could not transform.

WAY 30 The Fear of Intimacy

Every fight, competition, separation, role, feeling of deadness, judgement or grievance contains within it the fear of intimacy.

This means that the fear of intimacy is the root of some problems and an ingredient in most. Because we feel that we aren't adequate for the closeness of intimacy, we create problems to keep a certain distance. We feel that if someone really got to know us they wouldn't like us because they'd know how bad or inadequate we were. Fusion and sacrifice are ego traps that look like intimacy but are counterfeit because they still keep the distance between us and others. We can even use the fight with someone more distant from us to help keep a certain emotional distance between us and our partner. In other words, lack of bonding in our relationships signals outside traumas. The same thing can be said of problems. We use them as a way of distancing ourselves without appearing to separate ourselves from those around us.

Where there is separation there is fear, guilt and judgement. When we judge we separate from others, showing that we are superior to those we have judged. This sets up power struggle, competition, control and comparison, which are all ways of keeping us winning, losing, gloating, gleeful or suffering but never at the same level as another and never together with them. Only equality allows for intimacy and mutuality. Intimacy means we're not afraid to join and get close. Our ability to join with another in intimacy brings about some of the greatest enjoyment there is. The deepest levels of intimacy can lead to feelings of heaven on earth. These feelings can be so profound that they lead to momentary experiences of Oneness and enlightenment. Intimacy is one of the great gifts of life providing bonding and meaning. We achieve intimacy to the same extent we will achieve partnership and success.

Fear of intimacy is one of the great fears of humankind. It stops relationships and it prevents them from getting deeper. Intimacy is the willingness, courage, joining and commitment that brings relationships closer, healing a level of fear at the same time. In the Bible the idea that occurs most often is, 'Do not fear.' Everyone today speaks of the fear of commitment but this comes from the fear of intimacy and the belief that we are not worth the continuous attention of a long-term relationship. If you don't value yourself enough for intimacy and commitment, you won't be able to value others either.

So the trouble going on with someone in our life becomes a good excuse, a delay and a distraction not to join in intimacy with our partner or with anyone else.

Exercise

For this exercise, imagine the person closest to you. If you don't have a love partner, do this with your closest friend or family member. You can also do this with a potential true love on their way to you who has not yet arrived.

Imagine that this person is with you, but separate from you. This separation is as big as your fear of intimacy. How many steps are you apart? Ask yourself what scares you about the other, about the relationship, about intimacy. When you have your answer, ask yourself if you're willing to let this fear go to have them step closer. If you are, let go of the fear and see them take a step closer. As they take a step closer, ask yourself what scares you now about them. Whatever comes up, ask yourself if you're willing to let that go. If you're not willing to let that go, then feel and increase that fear until it begins to melt away. If new feelings come up that are too frightening to release, just continue to feel and exaggerate your feelings bit by bit, melting them away. In other words, by exaggerating the experience, you exorcise negative feelings so that those you do experience become insignificant and eventually disappear.

Though one of the easiest ways to get through a fear is just to let it go, one of the things that can help you is if you imagine an angel or a friend who has been an 'angel without wings' supporting you to let go of these feelings. This may be someone you know, or it may be a simple visualisation of an angel. Every time you let go, the person across from you will move forward until you both can embrace and join each other.

WAY 31 Getting or Getting Along

This chapter is once again about our attitudes, and how they affect our ability to get along with others. Our attitudes may be an aspect of ourselves that are holding us back, but they may be more hidden than evident. We have attitudes about many things. Some of these attitudes we hide from ourselves, such as the attitude about our direction in life, which comes from making many choices in the same direction. Sometimes we do not know that we've even made choices until we are faced with the results.

Basically we have the choice between *getting* or *getting along*. When presented with this choice, most of us would confirm that we want to get along; however, whenever we have trouble with others, a need to 'get something' underpins the problem. The person with whom we are not getting along seems to be obstructing us from doing or getting what we want in some way, or making us angry by what they do. We don't realise that this attitude is an indication that we want something – want to get something – even if it is as simple as wanting to get them out of our way. We don't want them to hold on to us; instead, we want them to share their abundance, and not to deprive us of what we feel we deserve. If we feel that someone is depriving us, we get angry and demand what is rightfully ours. We want them to change for us. We want them to do it our way rather than their way.

The alternative is to find a common way where we can take a step towards maturity, where we can heal ourselves, where we could give more, where we could let go of the *judgement* that is causing our upset, where we could learn what would really make us happy. If we keep demanding we will not be happy even if the demand is met at this particular time. A fight stems from demanding a need that is not being fulfilled. Usually the very thing we demand is what we are called upon to give in the situation. It takes a certain willingness, which is what positive attitude is all about, for us to take responsibility to get along rather than to expect the other to do all of the shifting.

Getting along is something that is required over and over again in a love relationship where both parties will be asked to change many times, always to become more mature and more of their true selves for the relationship to be successful. As we move forward, we become more mature and less reactive. We evolve as people, and our relationships subsequently evolve. If one partner, or someone with whom we're fighting, takes a true step forward to another level of success, *both* sides benefit and step forward. This is a relationship principle and shows the economy of relationships. When we have stepped forward everyone around us benefits. We become more mature, successful, loving, able to receive and be happy and our partner receives the benefit of this as well. Similarly, if we get stuck with the attitude of getting, taking or even attacking then we won't suffer alone. Everyone we love will be affected by and pay the price of our recalcitrance and bad attitudes. With our attitudes we head towards either 'getting' or 'getting along', towards either death or life.

Our willingness or commitment to learn to 'get along', to heal ourselves along the way, will show us each conflict or judgement that needs to be addressed for us to move forward. We can ask for grace and heaven's help each step of the way. It is our higher mind's job to heal these problems, by healing the fear that underlies each one, if we would just allow it.

So we have to decide whether we will learn, grow and heal and move toward life or whether we will stay stuck, judgmental, righteous, attacking, locked in our suffering, and heading for death. The conflict we don't resolve as we move through life is the one that can kill us. The problem with someone with whom we are not getting along represents one of life's lessons. If it is a dark, painful lesson, our ego has got involved. If it is a lesson of love, freedom, light and mutuality, it is God's lesson for the situation. We can always choose our direction in life, and there are basically only two directions. One is towards life and living, and the other is towards death.

We don't have to work out how to resolve a problem or conflict. Our desire to have it resolved, our willingness to have it resolved, our commitment to have it resolved is our contribution to the resolution of the situation. If we have this attitude no one will be our scapegoat for a conflict that we have inside. No one will be held hostage to our fear of going forward. We will attack or sue no one to hold ourselves back. We will actually feel grateful they showed us this buried piece within ourselves that was suffering and in conflict. And by our positive attitude the way will be presented to us to solve the problem because we are moving in the right direction and open to solution.

Exercise

Choose your direction. Will it be towards life or death? Will you choose rebellion and revenge or love and happiness? Will you fight, which is only fighting yourself or will you give up the fight to be at peace? It is only your judgement that keeps you from peace. Remember you're not choosing for yourself alone. Will you choose healing, pain, learning and stepping forward or righteousness, suffering, dark lessons and being stuck? Our suffering is our responsibility and we can change it through our choice.

Today, be willing, or at least be willing to be willing, to free yourself. What do you want and choose? Will this be one more lesson on the way to success or that which stops you forever? Ask for the grace to make this easy.

WAY 32 Paying off Guilt

Our egos are made up of guilt and fear. With guilt comes the self-punishment and self-attack with which the ego keeps itself strong. The way our minds work is that all of us have guilt and, because of that guilt, we punish ourselves. The ego, made up of guilt and other negative emotions and self-concepts, uses guilt to separate us from others. The ego is built on the principle of separation and uses it to keep us from joining in friendships, partnership and love. The ego fosters domination, competition, winning at any price and trying to prove it is superior to others. On the other hand, the ego seeks to suffer, lose or be inferior, thus gaining 'dark glamour'. Glamour comes from being the best or the worst, which reinforces our specialness. The nature of guilt is that while it keeps us stuck and withdrawn, having built a monument to a mistake, it desperately craves specialness.

We all feel guilt and it is always a mistake. A mistake is something we can correct. Guilt is something for which we punish ourselves, or bury and project out onto others, seeing them at fault and worthy of punishment. Innocent people do not blame or see sin. They just see a call for help.

A victim situation is an ego strategy to pay off guilt by punishing ourselves. Actually, becoming a victim never works to lessen guilt, but only increases it. As a victim, we feel bad as a result of the pain and bad for being victimised. Feeling bad is the nature of guilt. Anything about which we feel bad we feel a sense of guilt. In a victim situation, the guilt is increased for both the victim and the victimiser. With guilt, we either become more withdrawn or we continue to victimise, or to be the victim. There are further ego strategies to get rid of the pain and the guilt and, of course, they only compound it.

Any feelings that are unresolved from the past, such as sadness, loss, hurt, rejection or heartbreak, now have an added aspect of guilt tied in with them, since we still have the pain which feels bad, and we also feel bad about what happened. This is just one of the ways the ego keeps itself and the sense of separation strong because this pain and guilt within us is a wedge between us and others.

Back in 1976, I helped three women, in the easiest possible way, out of physically abusive situations in one session apiece. By this time I had already discovered the hidden or subconscious parts of the mind that play a big part in our victim situations. With the first woman, I had the inspiration to check to see if there wasn't something about which she was punishing herself. Sure enough, there was a big misunderstanding from childhood for which she was punishing herself. When we cleared up the misunderstanding, the self-abusive part of her disappeared and her husband miraculously quit abusing her. In the next two weeks, I had two similar clients and got similar results. Clearing the misunderstandings of guilt, especially from childhood, is one of the most important factors in helping people with major illness regain their health.

Do not mistake the intent of this essay. I am not implying that it is the victim's fault for being victimised, nor do I mean to exonerate the abuser. My intention is to free us all from the mistaken and catastrophic effects of guilt. To do this we must give up the blame-guilt cycle and to take responsibility for our lives and our experiences. There is no excuse for abuse except in the ego's plan. Yet we are all responsible for victim-victimiser situations that we are in or those that occur around us. If it is around us then it is a part of our collective story, a part of our belief system, a part of the mirror of our mind that reflects a conspiracy against ourselves. We are all 100 percent responsible and we are all 100 percent innocent for everything that surrounds us, everything in our world. Innocence is the only way lasting change can occur.

These are the principles that we can use to help us heal ourselves and to move forward out of guilt and victim situations.

1. Recognise we have been doing the best we can and that we can do better.
2. Take 100 percent responsibility for the situation.
3. Realise that if there has been a negative situation, we have probably used it to attack ourselves out of some mistaken guilt from the past.
4. Choose to find the guilt and forgive ourselves and everyone involved in the past situation.

Remember if we still have a grievance against anyone, it points to hidden guilt which needs to be resolved. When we have reached innocence, we will see everyone that way.

5. Forgive everyone in the present situation including ourselves and God.

Exercise

Examine your present situation. Choose to be responsible but innocent. Even if you feel bad about something, realise that it is just a mistake and that the guilt will only keep you from changing. Resolve to change and be free of this situation. You can exaggerate and feel all the guilt until it is 'burned away'. It is a slow but sure and effective way of getting rid of the guilt.

If the situation has a bad feeling involved, examine it as some form of self-attack. Notice that you probably had this particular bad feeling before. Experience it again. See what situations from the past come to your mind. In all the situations that come to your mind, forgive yourself and everyone present.

Ask yourself:

If I were to know when the guilt that is at the root of this problem began, it was probably when I was at the age of _____

If I were to know who was involved, it was probably

_____

If I were to know what happened that this mistaken guilt began, it was probably _____

Once again, forgive yourself and everyone present in this root situation.

Now ask your higher mind, your creative mind, to carry you and everyone back to their centres within themselves. This is a place of peace, innocence, bonding and grace. See what effect this has on the situation . . . If the situation is not yet completely happy for everyone, ask to be carried back to a second centre. If it is not completely happy and loving and filled with light there, ask that everyone be carried back to a third centre. If the scene is not yet fully resolved, ask to be carried back to a fourth centre. You can go through succeeding centres until the whole situation turns completely to light.

WAY 33 Self-Attack

Let's imagine for a moment that anyone who ever attacked you, hurt you, put you down or slighted you, didn't exist. In their place imagine, if you will, that there are remote control robots and that you have the remote control in your hand. Every time you thought someone else attacked you, you find an entry in your remote control recorder of when you activated this robot to attack yourself.

Does this sound strange or absurd to you? Actually it is whimsical only in a literal sense, metaphorically it is exactly what happens. If I had to choose the biggest problem that most of us share in this world, based on my thirty years' experience, I would have to say that it's self-attack. Every negative or painful incident we ever experienced was at some level a form of self-attack. It is the most chronic problem in the world. We are all so hard on ourselves, which means that in the long or short run we will also then be hard on others. If we were not being so hard on ourselves there would be no victims or victimisers.

Subconsciously, someone with whom we are not getting along reflects a part of us that we have judged, split off and repressed. Yet this part is still within us and it seems to be attacking us. This part appears to have another agenda with goals different to the ones that we have, and this is now reflected by the outside situation with this person with whom we're having a hard time.

Self-attack comes from separation, authority conflict, fear, guilt for what we did or didn't do, feelings of failure or valuelessness, especially in regard to our families and, at the deepest level, guilt for failing to live our purpose, embrace our destiny and rejoin with God. Every worry or fearful thought is an attack against ourselves.

We have even projected out self-judgement and self-attack on God, seeing the highest force of love and mercy as being judgmental and angry.

Basically, if we could see ourselves as loveable and let ourselves be loved, the world would be changed for the better. If we could stop attacking ourselves, we could have heaven on earth. Not one of the reasons for which we are actually attacking ourselves is true. Self-attack is literally a form of indulgence and sacrifice in a form we turn against ourselves. Self-attack is ultimately a form of rebellion and revenge against our partners, our parents and God. It is a lethal form of pouting and tantrum. If we stopped our self-attack our lives would correspondingly be problem-free, as it is one of the key dynamics present in any problem. Now is the time to make another choice, to give up the fight we have against ourselves not only for our sakes but for the sake of everyone we love.

It is time to realise that even though we feel guilty and have condemned ourselves, it is not the ultimate truth. Guilt is a psychological mistake, a trap of the ego that we use to build separation and dark glamour.

It's a symptom of fear in hiding. The ultimate truth is innocence and pure love.

Commit to the truth. It is time to ask to be shown our innocence. If God, the principle of innocence, sees us as innocent, why is this not the truth? If we were created as innocent by God, we could only *imagine* or perceive that our innocence had changed. It could not occur in reality. The innocent can only see innocence; the rest they recognise as a call for help. Isn't it somewhat arrogant on our part to see ourselves as guilty if God sees us as innocent? Only innocence learns the lesson and changes for everyone's benefit, while guilt imagines it has an excuse to stay stuck and not change.

Exercise

Make two lists. In one, list those things about which you feel guilty. In the other, list those things for which you are attacking yourself. For each item in both lists commit to your innocence. Now, beside each 'self-attack' listing, write down who this self-attack is an attack against, besides yourself of course. Besides yourself, against whom do you have a grievance? Ask yourself and write down what grievance you have against them, which is hiding underneath your attack. Remember, too, that self-attack is another form of attack on others, and another way that shows that there is a grievance against someone else lurking beneath the surface. Grievance is the miracle that could free you and everyone. If you let go of the grievance and self-attack you can receive the miracle.

Spend five minutes, three times today, just watching the

thoughts go through your mind. After every negative or fearful thought say to yourself 'This thought shows a place where I am attacking myself. I chose to do this no longer, and to love myself.'

WAY 34 Unfinished Business and Transformational Communication

We have spoken about unfinished business from the past interfering with the present. Now it is time to examine this in a bit more detail. There is a term called 'transference', which refers to the fact that in any situation where there are problems, there is a carry-over of feelings, problems and unfinished relationships from the past. This means that if we are *not* enjoying love, joy, creativity and abundance, we are trying to heal the past in the present and that our present problems are actually past ones in disguise. If we have the awareness that upsetting feelings are just unfinished pain from the past, we will be both more motivated and more able to understand how to heal the situation in the present. For example, if as a woman we have an unhealed situation with our father, it can affect our relationships with our brothers, boyfriend, friends, bosses, husband, and sons. While these are the most common relationships affected by father issues, carry-over feelings with our fathers can occur with any of our ongoing relationships.

The implications of this concept can be staggering because it means that everything that is not love is transference. Our adult heartbreaks go back to childhood heartbreaks as our adult failures go back to childhood failures. Situations in our lives now actually reflect a number of relationships, both past and present. This means that unfinished healing issues we had with our families while growing up will have an effect on our entire lives. As we forgive those people from the past it can have a transformative effect on our lives now and if we forgive people in our present life it will have an ameliorating effect on our relationships from the past.

When we have some upset – which is unfinished business in the present – we can ask ourselves: 'To what relationship or situation does this refer from my past'? This gives us an added dimension for healing when we realise that when we are trying to get needs met in the present relationship, they are actually unmet needs from the past. This is what makes the extra stress and pressure on our present communication and relationship now, because we are not only talking to someone in the present, but also to someone from the past. No wonder communication gets confused at times. Understanding transference also allows us to become more accountable for present situations because it lets us realise that we have brought our past into the present for healing. This is one of the reasons for manifesting this present situation or issue with our present problem person.

Exercise

One of the best ways to resolve situations or issues with problem people is through communication. Even if it may not be appropriate to communicate at this deep a level with someone with whom you are having a problem, it is extremely helpful to understand this principle. First, the communication can begin by setting a goal as to what you want to occur as the result of the communication. All through the communication, especially if it seems to take a downturn for the worse, reset the goal you want to occur. Secondly, take responsibility for your feelings. If you think someone made you feel something, you don't understand how feelings come from within us. Our feelings are our responsibility. They come from choices we make in reaction to certain events, even though it seems like someone else made us feel it. Negative emotions come from some kind of judgement we made. If our feelings are negative we have typically been carrying them inside ourselves for a while. Our ego looks for new events to compound our pain while our higher mind looks for a place to heal the old pain inside.

In your communication, commit to and support both of you winning. Share with the other what's not working for you with an attitude of responsibility for your feelings, thoughts and perception.

Once you've shared what isn't working for you, talk about what you are feeling and experiencing. Take responsibility for your feelings and ask for the other's support. Do not expect them to have to change because you have certain feelings. Share your feelings and clarify your experience around the event. They may also spontaneously share their experience. Never blame in attitude, tone or words, it's just a form of attack. Communication stops when blame begins. It's a signal that you've become afraid to step forward and are using the attack, fight or judgement to cover your fear and to try to control them to get your way. Don't use your feeling to stop yourself. Use them to help free both yourself and them.

After they share or clarify, to take the communication to a deeper level, be conscious of your feelings around the situation. Share your feelings as deeply as possible and then reflect on events from earlier in your life that led to these feelings. While you may tell your partner the story, emphasise what you were feeling. Sometimes a story doesn't emerge, just deeper, older but familiar feelings. If you do not attack your partner by displacing your old feelings from the past on them now, they will typically be motivated to support you. Paradoxically, the more you share all these bad feelings, the better you feel, having freed yourself from either the pattern itself or a layer of the pattern by your communication. As you learn to share like this, you build your confidence in your ability to communicate and bring yourself from turmoil to peace. This type of sharing frees you and the person with whom the feeling came up.

If it is inappropriate to share with this person because of a work situation, ask a friend to role-play the problem person for you as best they can. By following the principle of transformational communication you can heal yourself of the past that is trying to be healed in the present.

WAY 35 We Reap What We Sow

In any relationship, it is evident that we reap what we sow, in spite of any complaints to the contrary. Of course sacrifice, dependency, or giving to take, don't count as forms of giving and they thwart or sabotage our ability to receive. So many times we show a sweet, innocent side to the world, complaining how we have been victimised terribly in some relationship. This 'outside' nice, sweet character hides an attacking, aggressive 'inside', which we sometimes deny even to ourselves.

Besides our hidden attack on others, we are also filled with self-attack that is a destructive force in our lives. While on the surface we act benignly, within us there are all kinds of dark stories, shadow figures and conflicts that we project out onto others. These are all aspects of ourselves, and although they are hidden, they set up trouble in our lives. Every judgement and grievance we have generates a problem. As such, each problem we have shows a hidden or not-so-hidden attack, judgement or grievance.

All of this is just an example of reaping what we are sowing. There are similar principles to this in the subconscious mind that are actually built on this law, such as: 'No one can do anything to us that we are not already doing to ourselves.' And 'No one can do

anything to us we are not already doing to others.'
Whenever we attempt to attack or do anything negative to anyone, we do it to ourselves, too. We are
going either to sink together or swim together and we
get the choice. There's another important principle at
work here, and that is 'We do to those around us what
we do to ourselves.' So if we attack ourselves we also
will end up attacking those close to us. All of these
principles led me to re-invent an ancient proverb a
few years ago, which is 'People who live in a house
of mirrors should not throw stones'. Anything we do
to others we do to ourselves and anything we do to
ourselves we do to others.

When we see any negativity in our world that is
creating hardship, we can begin to look for the hidden
part of our consciousness that it reflects. Once they
have started to look for their dissociated dark side,
I've known people have it come to them in a dream,
a book they were reading, or a TV show they saw.
Sometimes the buried part came to them by what
someone else said, or sometimes it just popped into
their minds in such a way that they knew what had
popped in was the root of their problem.

Once you find the root of your problem you can
make another choice about what it is you want. You
can always ask for grace and the help of heaven or
your higher mind. You can ask that your root fear that
has generated the problem with this person disappears
or you can let go of attack for peace. All of this will
begin the process of healing and transformation.

Exercise

Take the person with whom you're having a hard time; they can be of service to you to help you find a self you judged, broke off and repressed. Ask yourself and guess intuitively:

If I were to know, who was present when I judged this part of myself it was _____

If I were to know, what was going on, it was _____

If I were to know what's happened in my life as a result of choices I made back at this time, it was _____

What I would like to choose now to change the decisions I made then is _____

Find the part or parts of yourself you judged in that situation. Love those young 'selves' until they grow up to your present age and melt back into you.

Let heaven pour love through you for those selves to grow up. Now let yours and heaven's love pour out to the people in the original painful scene so that the selves in them that are both in pain and causing pain, will begin to grow up and melt back into them, bringing more confidence and wholeness.

Imagine the dark ideas represented by the other. How many of these dark selves do you have? Let them all melt together into a giant one. This giant show is holographic, a 3-D projection. Step into it. Look around, you will find a gateway to a part of your mind that was lost before. Go through the gateway. Find and enjoy what is there. In the rare case that the part of the mind you find is dark and scary, merely ask your higher mind to clean it up and bring light to this part of your mind.

WAY 36 Healing Control

Control is one of the singularly unattractive aspects that holds back both single and married people alike. No one wants a bossy, nagging, complaining partner. People will shy away when potential partners exhibit this trait. In any problem, control is one of the core dynamics. At some level, we are always seeking to control ourselves or someone else with our problems. Control is like going around with a chip on our shoulders. The more we have it, the more people want to fight or stay away from us, so they can have the freedom to do things their way. Control masquerades as competence but competence is attractive and rarely gets caught in fights.

Of course, not having a partner is a way of keeping control, a way of having things perpetually our way. We do not have to deal with another's wishes, desires or preferences. We do not have to fight anyone to keep ourselves safe or to get our way. We do not want to find a partner too interesting, attractive or loveable, because then we would lose control. We are afraid we would get hurt or go into sacrifice just like in the past. So we choose safe partners and the safest partner is none at all.

In a relationship, control is mistaking our way for the best way. After the honeymoon period, our control gets us into power struggles with our partners.

Later, it leads to deadness in the relationship as we seek to withdraw enough so that the other cannot control us. We also withdraw to keep control of the negative, buried emotions that turn up for healing as we move to join our partners, so we tend to stay away from them. Because we do not know how to deal with these emotions, we keep them buried as best we can.

In relationships, control can be used in any area where the body is used, such as affection, sex or health. When control invades these areas of a relationship, the relationship is in danger. All too often I have dealt with people who used sex or health as a part of a fight to control their partners, not realising that their partner was backing away from them so as not to be controlled. If one partner was backing away from something like sex which they valued a great deal, so as not to be controlled, then that same partner would also be typically withdrawing in areas of romance, affection, communication, sharing, or other areas equally important to their controlling partner. Partners, especially men, do not mind being motivated by sex, especially if what they are being motivated towards is something that builds the relationship, but that same partner will resist being 'controlled' by sex, even if it is their favourite thing. Joining, communicating, or any form of bridge-building are enormously effective ways of ending the power struggles and deadness, which come from the different forms of control.

Control comes from fear, especially the fear of getting hurt, which speaks of unresolved heartbreaks. We control in an attempt to prevent being hurt, or to prevent others being hurt. It is an attempt to get ours and everyone else's needs met as we perceive them. But it is an attempt to do this our way, which sets up power struggles with everyone around us. Those who go along with our way of doing things and let themselves be dominated become 'boring' in our eyes, because the relationship is so unequal. Any fight or disagreement we have with anyone points to conflict and control in ourselves. Any boredom we have with another speaks of our control. All power struggles also point to a place of trying to get our way.

The opposite of control is peace, integration, communication, confidence and trust. Trust is putting our whole mind behind something, knowing that it will turn out fine. Control is where we have lost faith in our partners, ourselves and the situation and seek to use some form of force, threat, manipulation or coercion to keep them in line. If we are faithless to our partner in this way, they will be similarly faithless to us. Without confidence, all we are left with is control and the fights and withdrawals they engender.

Every time we are trying to control, it reflects our split mind, which was fractured when we were heartbroken. By projecting the more hidden sides of our mind onto others, we try to control them in a way that brings up the pain of the original fracture. This could be avoided if we integrated our positions so that a new level of confidence and success shows up. Another way of healing control is to go to such a deep level of peace that the conflict and old pain falls away. If we have faith in either our partners, ourselves or the situation, we have the confidence, which is both highly attractive and successful and obviates control.

Exercise

Imagine that the person with whom you are in a power struggle represents a part of your mind. Imagine that part this person represents and the part your self or your position represents melting down into each other so that there is a big pile of melted energy. Now, join these piles together in a way that will contain the best of both worlds. If there is any negative feeling left over, integrate that feeling into what has already been melted together along with your higher mind. Keep doing this with your higher mind and what has already been integrated if there is any negative bit left over at all. This can heal many layers of conflict all at once.

Today put your trust into your current relationship with the person with whom you are not getting along. Know that it will come out perfectly. Every time you think of it, return once again to this confident knowing. If you are too frightened to have faith, ask your higher mind to remove the fear you have. When you know it is all going to turn out fine, it does. Confidence is charismatic and attractive. It helps whether the problem is with a current partner or someone around you. It is this confidence that can take you to the next step.

Ask yourself intuitively, how many layers of peace you would have to reach to have the conflict fall away. Now relax and ask your higher mind to carry you to a level of peace. When that is achieved ask your higher mind to carry you to a deeper level of peace. When this is accomplished ask once again. Continue going to deeper levels of peace until you have reached that part of your mind in peace deeper than the conflict. It will then disappear.

WAY 37 Competition is a Form of Delay

Competition is interconnected with attachment, the basis of all pain. Competition comes about through separation, which also generates fear, need, attachment, indulgence, every idol that we see as a source of our happiness.

Competition actually hides fear of the next step. Winning over your opponent becomes the consuming desire so that the real issue is not faced. Success is actually avoided in competition, or becomes secondary to winning. Winning is not synonymous with success. In winning, what needs to be learned to generate success can be missed. Success is a much fuller experience. It implies levels of partnership and real achievement of true goals, ones that will support future ease, success and partnership rather than the driven quality that seems to come from winning. Success faces forward and finds what needs to be integrated so that everyone can win. Winning brings down the one with whom we are competing or the one with whom we are in conflict, thinking that 'besting' them will somehow give us what we need. Winning can become obsessive and short-sighted, whereas success doesn't rest on its laurels but looks forward to learning and change as prerequisites. Winning can lull us into thinking that there is nothing to change. If when we lose in the win-lose cycle we concentrate on learning, not on how to win but on how to succeed, we progress to a new level.

Competition begins in an unbonded family. The fear, scarcity and separation dictate certain family roles, which are both personal compensations and an attempt to balance the family. But these defences have no success and at best can only maintain the present family dilemma. At the bottom of everything lies the fear of loss that begets scarcity and competition.

Competition is a defence that actually creates what it attempts to prevent. Competition keeps generating a fear of loss even if you win. It also ignores the only source of true success, which is integration and co-operation. Years ago the visionary Buckminster Fuller demonstrated that, if the whole world co-operated, within 10 years the poorest person would be richer than the richest person today. Yet we ignore what is evident. Only through interdependence and recognising the mutuality of interests can we have any long-lasting success.

Competition is a way of trying to win by turning others into objects in order to support a certain grandiose self-concept of ourselves. We are always attempting to be legends in our own minds. Any time we objectify another to meet our needs, we objectify and dissociate ourselves. This turns a potentially joyful situation into one of mere indulgence, which does not allow receiving. Joy has been lost in the scramble for glee and proving one's superiority. Of course, what one is trying to prove is what one doubts about oneself, so the vicious circle of win-lose continues unabated. In competition, winning is never enough, because self-concepts are built on self-doubts. Joy can only be found in joining. Once the power relationships have to transform us and move us toward confidence and wholeness is recognised, an attitude that values these healing conflicts begins to take hold, and we move toward partnership, co-creativity and unity. In other words, once we realise how powerful relationships can be to move us forwards towards confidence and wholeness, then we have a better attitude and will achieve everything we need for peace and happiness. Success begins to be viewed according to our success with others. The greater the mutuality, the greater the success.

In competition we are seeking to meet our needs through others, and others are seeking to meet their needs through us. When someone loses it is only a matter of time before they seek to ambush us so they can win. If we keep winning, our partners will become dependent, unattractive and passive-aggressive. Yet this obscures the fact that if one of us were to take the next step, both would be moved forward to a new plateau, a new integration and understanding where both could win together. There is no relationship in trouble that does not have some form of competition. Competition insidiously destroys relationships.

After all, don't you think you are really a better person than the person with whom you're not getting along? Aren't you, at the very least, a morally superior person? Aren't you consoling yourself with this? You may therefore think winning over another person is natural and justified. Yet this type of thinking will affect every relationship we have, including our closest relationships. For every relationship in which we are competing is actually a subconscious reflection of the competition in our primary relationship.

Competition generates power struggle, subtly or otherwise, and it also generates deadness in a relationship. The deadness is merely a withdrawal reflecting the underlying fight going on. By recognising deadness, a couple can get in touch with areas in which they have compromised or adjusted to the other, but not come to resolution and mutuality. Deadness is a way of withdrawing to keep from losing in competition.

A less understood form of competition, yet one that is no less deadly in its delay, is attachment. Only through attachment can we feel hurt or disappointed. Our attachment is a form of need. It may be some form of taking. It is a counterfeit form of love that easily leads to hurt. Love feels only poignancy and birthing as our hearts grow. Hurt comes only when we lose something to which we have been attached, or when we reject the way someone is acting by believing that they are not meeting our needs.

There are two aspects of competition in attachment. One is using others to get our needs met. The second aspect is not sharing what we have with others, having more of a certain thing or person than anyone else. It is this that is the basis of an attachment or the creation of an idol. When an attachment is lost or an idol falls, our dreams seem shattered and we fall into heartbreak and disillusionment. This disappointment is what tempts us to die. It is the pain of this loss that hinders our evolution.

At one level, growth could be seen as moving through one disillusionment after another, or at least as surrendering one attachment after another. When we are disillusioned, a certain self-concept that was built on being better than someone is shattered. We then feel wretched, valueless and like a failure. Yet these also are only self-concepts or compensations hiding the true goodness within us.

Competition is always quick to find fault and to correct others. Correction is a form of arrogance, which keeps us looking for mistakes in those around us rather than looking forward to see where our next step is. Whenever we are correcting another it is a sure sign that we are avoiding what needs correction in us. The best competition is not a competition at all but a desire to excel and expand personal or global horizons. We look on opponents as fellow players who help to call out the very best in us.

Exercise

Today, examine areas of competition in your life. Write down the self-concepts you are trying to prove about yourself. What self-concepts do these hide? When you discover major negative self-concepts, remember these too are merely concepts you are trying to prove to hide your true goodness and power. We hide our true goodness and power because we are afraid to be that good or to have it all out of fear of what might be expected of us. Discover and experience these truths about yourself.

Let go of all the self-concepts you discover. What you will have in its place is being or mastery.

The exercise can be done like this:
- *What this competition proves about me is* _____
- *What self-concept this one hides is* _____
- *And what self-concept this one hides is* _____

If you continue this exercise until completion you will go through some of your deepest, darkest shadows until you finally reach those filled with light and bliss.

Just keep writing down each reply that comes to you. Sometimes you'll have a feeling instead of an idea. If you do, this is the answer. If you don't know, then this also is a self-concept.

The Problem Person and
Our Relationship to
Ourselves

Our relationship to the problem person shows us our relationship to ourselves. The world is our mirror, showing us parts of our minds that we both like and dislike. All that we see shows us something that we have judged and with which we have dis-identified or disengaged in some way. Sometimes we judge something, project it out into the world, and then chase what we projected, because of the emptiness and neediness caused by pushing this quality away inside. We are attracted to people who represent the parts of ourselves that we repressed, but feel disapproval because we could not allow these character traits in ourselves.

There are other times when we judge and split off parts of ourselves, project them out on the world and judge outside us the wars we wage within, feeling separate and superior to this piece of ourselves as shown by someone in our world.

This idea may seem far-fetched, foolish, abstract or unhelpful. I guarantee that it is not any of those things. As a therapist, and marriage counsellor, business consultant and life coach, I assure you that this is one of the very practical concepts for healing and change that I have found in my thirty years of work.

The idea of perception being projection has helped me tens of thousands of times to help people change their world by changing their minds. If I can find the inner conflict that matches the outer conflict in their world then it is easy enough to help them change. Of course, at times there are many layers of obstructions or dynamics to heal. But in our world for every person we have a similar self-concept. This gives us a certain power and ability to change our minds and to change the world. I have seen relationships transform very quickly when the partners pull back their projection on each other, own it as a self-concept and do something to heal it that allows for a quick shift in the world.

'Everything is projection' or the recapitulation of our thoughts, wishes and beliefs of our mind on the world. Our problems and life disasters are what we think of as our sin or guilt projected out onto the world, so that it becomes a place of difficulty or self-attack for us.

Let me share with you an exercise that has helped many a relationship change in a very positive way.

Exercise

Name three qualities about the person with whom you are having a problem:

   1. _____

   2. _____

   3. _____

Now examine the first quality for your style in projecting.

Do you act out this same quality also, or would you rather die than ever do something like this? Do you vacillate between the two styles?

If you're the first style you can see that you do it, too. But if you have the second style you have denied, compensated and hidden this quality. The third style is a combination of the first two styles.

To help you with this second style you may want to find where it was that you judged and you fractured off this piece of you.

Ask yourself:

If I were to know when I judged this part of myself it was probably at the age of _____

If I were to know what occurred to cause me to judge and reject part of myself as 'bad,' it was _____

In this original situation feel yourself making a bridge of light to everyone. Do this with each person present until a level of bonding is established with everyone in that situation. It may take at least two to three times to restore the bonding in that past situation. You can now choose that all the compensations, which are acting in an opposite or positive way to hide the negative self-concepts inside, and all the negative self-concepts be integrated or melted together and then integrated back into you. This can help you if you have a lot of denial or reaction around a compensating style.

No matter what style you've had you will notice that there's been a lot of self-attack around this quality for yourself.

The important and final key is to ask yourself 'Do I

want to continue attacking myself or do I wish to help this person I've projected on?' If you decide to help them, let go of any self-attack around this quality and move past the separation between you. In your mind's eye imagine yourself reaching out and embracing them, extending your help.

Now move on to the second quality you have projected on the problem person.
- *Notice your style of either doing it also, compensating, or both.*
- *Notice how you torture yourself about this quality.*
- *Choose whether you wish to keep torturing yourself or whether you want to help the other.*
- *Imagine yourself letting the self-attack go and moving over to join them offering your support.*

Now complete this with the third quality or however many qualities are needed to be healed to see this 'problem person' in a completely different light.

WAY 39 Healing Negative Stories

In the deepest part of our minds, there are patterns that set the tone for our lives. These are the stories we are telling the world about ourselves. They give rise to both our waking and our sleeping dreams. Our everyday lives are made up of these stories. These stories come from idols, conspiracies, ego strategies and soul patterns. Idols are the people, places, things or situations outside us that we have made into false gods. We think they will save us and make us happy. Conspiracies are traps we set up so well it looks like we'll never get out of them. The dark stories that we tell about our lives try to achieve a certain result that we think will make us happy. These negative stories are so powerful that they can include people around us as players in our stories. Our soul patterns are the problems and issues we came to resolve in this life and a soul pattern usually shows itself by what happens in our original family. The ego can use our idols, conspiracies, soul patterns and dark stories to be a part of its strategy, which it promises will make us happy but never does.

Our stories, both dark and happy ones, come out of our deepest mind and determine what our lives are like and how we get along with others. If these stories take us in a negative direction, and we do not change them, they continuously bring up failure and pain.

Some of the more common negative stories are heart-break, fear, guilt, sacrifice, tragedy, soap opera, war, rebel, power struggle, death, tantrum, malice, evil, neediness, control, and revenge. Some of the healing stories are happiness, success, adventure, comedy, miracle, carefree, beautiful life, hero, spiritual odyssey, redemption and awakening.

As an example of a story that causes disruption in our relationships and keeps us from getting along with others, let us examine the example of a heartbreak story. You might have the best therapist in the world helping you heal your childhood and adult heartbreak pattern, but if he or she does not realise that there is even a deeper pattern of a heartbreak story going on, the heartbreaks will continue. This, of course, can have a major deleterious effect on how we get along with others.

There are three specific forms that a heartbreak story can take. It can come from something passed down inter-generationally, it can come from a painful story we are telling for some mistaken reason, or it can come from a 'past life' metaphor. We will examine this latter story in the chapter 'Karmic Stories' (see page 170).

We tell negative stories to experience something that we think will make us happy. We have made a plan for our happiness. The first and most important thing to realise is that our plan for happiness just does not work. It is put together by our ego – the principle of separation in our mind. This means that our ego will be frightened of love, creativity, abundance, and happiness. It tries to build itself up, win or lose, gain control, make itself indispensable to us so that we identify ourselves with our ego. If it accomplishes this, it makes us guard our specialness, zealously protecting itself against any perceived slights.

The purposes of the negative stories we tell about our lives are to get something, to attack ourselves, to have an excuse, to try to protect ourselves from certain fears, to pay off guilt, to control someone or ourselves, to defeat someone, to prove something, or to get revenge on someone. At times, these strategies work, but they never work to make us happy and that is our biggest mistake.

Inter-generational stories, pain, negative patterns and even predilection for certain diseases are passed down through the family. This inheritance begins with a certain trauma that occurred in one generation, and is passed on as unresolved emotional or physical symptoms, generation after generation, until someone in the family heals it and frees the family.

We will now work to free ourselves from these negative stories, which can play such a major part in how well we get along with anyone. A dark story within means we will be at odds not only with those around us but with ourselves as well.

Exercise

In the following exercises, you can either work with yourself intuitively, or you can ask your higher mind for the major story that is causing you trouble to show itself in the next day or week in an easy and recognisable way. Also ask yourself, how many negative stories of this kind are affecting you now? Once you realise the negative stories you have going, you can choose to let these go. Or, you can ask your higher mind to remove them and replace them with the gift that they have been hiding. Once you have discovered what dark stories you have, the following exercise can help you understand why you chose them and help you get rid of them.

It can be very helpful to come to the understanding of the strategies that you have for any story, and why you wanted a negative story. Once you realise the strategies have never worked for you, you can let go of these stories as a bad deal.

Ask yourself intuitively or just guess the answers to the following questions. If you think about the questions rather than just guessing the first thing that comes to your mind, your ego has stopped you from getting your answers and typically supplied ones of its own. Of course, you will not be stopped unless you want to be stopped from getting your true answers.

If I were to know what I was trying to get by having this story, it's probably _____

If I were to know what fear I was trying to protect myself from, it's probably _____

If I were to know what guilt I was trying to pay off, it's probably _____

If I were to know whom I was trying to defeat, it's probably _____

If I were to know whom I was trying to control and what it was about, it's probably _____

If I were to know how this was meant to hide my life purpose, it was probably _____

If I were to know what I was trying to prove, it's probably _____

If I were to know what excuse I was looking for, it's probably _____

If I were to know why I was trying to attack myself, it's probably _____

If I were to know on whom, beside myself, I was trying to get revenge, it's probably _____

If I were to know on to what or whom I was trying to hold, it was probably _____

Even though some of these answers will ring stronger than others, these dynamics will all be going on at the same time. You can choose to let go all of these strategies as a big mistake and a bad investment and you can do the same with your dark stories, asking that love, success or happy stories be put in their place.

Ask yourself what negative stories, and how many, are being passed down through your mother's side of the family. Then ask the same thing about your father's side of the family.

As an example, let's say there are three guilt stories and two heartbreak stories and one sacrifice story passed through your father's side of the family, and four control, three fear, two heartbreak and one sacrifice story being passed through your mother's side.

Now imagine your father standing before you. Within you are not only all these negative stories that you inherited but also the gifts to dissolve them. Reach deep inside and open the door in your mind to the gift or gifts that you have brought in to save your father and your ancestors from these guilt stories. Allow these gifts to wash through you, and then fill your father with them. When he is filled with these gifts, his guilt story is released. Then see, feel or sense these gifts passing back through each succeeding generation until all of your ancestors are free.

Then go to the next negative story with your father. Repeat the same exercise until your father is free. Then complete this exercise with your mother.

You came to free yourself and your ancestors and enjoy all of the gifts they have passed down to you.

WAY 40 Bonding and Societal Shifts

World society, in all its competitiveness, is poised on the brink of discovering the importance of bonding and partnerships, and this discovery will save us. The final stage of independence, to which Western society has evolved, is where most individuals died a generation ago. The effects of the last stages of independence are sacrifice, exhaustion, hard work, sacrifice, struggling just to keep up, deadened feelings, deadened sexuality, fear of intimacy, fear of success and living out of roles, rules and duties. All of our roles are compensations for feelings of failure. In this stage political correctness, which is living by form rather than authenticity, becomes a way of life. We feel depressed, burnt-out, over-busy, or in rarer cases, lazy. We work hard, secretly embracing difficulty yet nobly fighting against it to prove our value. When we become worn out from our roles, the feeling of failure emerges along with death temptations. We get trapped in dead relationships, no relationships, or triangle relationships.

At this stage, competitiveness has become an art form, but we do not realise that we use it to hide fear and to avoid the next step. We put our focus on winning rather than stepping forward to a new level of success. With competition, we try to win or withdraw so as not to lose, all the time being frightened of intimacy and partnership that is the only way forward. In the US, the Republicans and Democrats of the Clinton era vividly acted out in American politics this dead zone stage of competitiveness, and the trap and bankruptcy of it. All of this is a fear of stepping forward to change and a new way of living that fosters partnership, success and closeness.

The next step that we can make individually and collectively, is that of partnership, co-operation and collective success so that we can live in the intimacy of things and people and truly enjoy our lives. Once we've finally realised the empty posturing of independence, having gone down that road as far as we can, we graduate into interdependence. When more and more of us have made this choice, there will be a shift in consciousness of unprecedented proportions, along with a massive change in our way of relating and being together. When we see there is a better way of living, such as partnership, mutuality, shared success, friendship, responsiveness, co-operation and bonding, we find that we can let layer after layer of the deadness fall away. We then move through the doubt the ego throws at us as its last defence to stop us from accepting the ethic of bonding and co-operation. We begin to step up, explore, research, examine and finally choose the new way. We discover the truth, that success and intimacy require our wholehearted commitment and authenticity.

When we live independently and only for ourselves we do not know the sense of ease and freedom that comes with partnership and bonding as the key ethic. Mutuality, helping and friendship then become a way of life. We are willing to enjoy the fruits of leadership as we are called to help those around us. In so doing, we embrace our gifts of reason, intelligence, awareness, humour, spontaneity, inspiration, intuition, attraction, allurement, charisma, brilliance, buoyancy, irresistibility, luck and many more. Finally, through partnership, we can receive and enjoy again. Life becomes easy and there is a new flow of anticipated abundance.

The level of humour, reward, tenderness, success, playfulness and fun that occurs at this level regenerates us. The world becomes new again with an outlook of friends helping friends instead of the hidden, or not-so-hidden competitiveness, fear and separateness that keeps society, families and relationships in bondage rather than bonding. All of this separateness comes from the separation, fear and lack of unbonded families, passed down generation after generation, keeping us crippled emotionally, creatively and in relationships. Yet we are at a place just before a change of consciousness. We have the possibility to leap forward to unheralded levels of prosperity and peace that come about through mutuality and teamwork. Each one of us that commits to partnership and bonding helps us all move forward. This will allow us to work co-operatively and efficiently – this means we work smarter rather than harder. Bonding naturally gives us more balance with family and career. It is a future where everyone has a place and everyone can win.

Exercise

Today, choose with your whole heart and mind that you will live by partnership, bonding and friendship. Make these the goals of your life and the key principles by which you live.

Don't worry about the future and whether you will be able to succeed at your goals. This first, significant choice is the most crucial. As we go forward in life and relationships there will be lessons and calls for new commitment, but it is important to begin by committing now to this goal. Keep this principle always in mind, especially when there is a problem. Ask yourself, what can I do to make things better? How can I be a better friend, a better partner? How can we both win?

Say to yourself with power and feeling, 'I choose that there be partnership, bonding and friendship in my life. I live by mutuality for everyone's success.'

This is particularly important to do if you have any conflicts or problems. Take a few minutes, close your eyes, and see what solution comes to you. Your higher mind always has a way for everyone to win. Allow your mind to become peaceful enough for it to come to you. Ask for the truth. Desire the truth with all your heart. Only an ego investment would keep you in conflict when there is a way for you both to succeed. This commitment helps us move through the problems that now confront our lives and relationships and their resolution turns into the wisdom that we can use to help others who are also learning these lessons.

WAY 41 The Shadow Figure

A shadow is an aspect, quality or belief about ourselves that we hate. These self-concepts can occur in
our lives when we mistakenly judge and split off a
part of ourselves that we feel 'sinned'. Then we repress
it and to keep away from the guilt that stems from
it, we project it out on the world around us. We make
many 'nice', 'good', 'conformist', 'hard-working' roles
to cover and compensate for these negative self-
concepts or shadows. This doesn't allow us to receive
from the goodness or hard work these selves accomplish because they are actually a defence and not true
giving. These compensations, which are there to prove
we really are good, lead to sacrifice, and feelings of
deadness and burnout.

The ego builds itself on these roles and shadow
figures, which contain guilt, fear and separation. Here
is a classic example of how the ego works. When we
are young and we separate from our parents, the ego
has us believe that we killed our parents and stole their
gifts, because of our lost bonding. This gives us shadow
figures of 'failure', 'thief', 'murderer', 'orphan',
'betrayer' and 'rebel'. We then repress these shadows
but still attack ourselves for them. The self-attack
comes from the guilt that hides under our pain or
grievances about the lost bonding. Not being able to
stand the guilt about ourselves, we pass it off or project

it onto others both far and near, judging them for what is inside us.

All of us have many shadow figures. Here are a few typical ones besides the ones already mentioned that have come up fairly often over the years: destroyer, black widow, fool, devil woman, pervert, abuser, betrayer, destroyer, rebel, invalid, sad sack, dark goddess, bureaucrat, torturer, undoer, invader, tyrant, Hitler, bastard, bitch, taker, user, seducer, rapist, thug, stupid, bully, coward, manipulator, vampire, bureaucrat, Mafia, controller, monster, psychopath, sociopath, weakling, soul-less, zombie, toxic person and many more. A shadow figure can be any person.

Not being able to stand these self-concepts, we attack them constantly within us and are frightened of them in dreams or in life. If we perceive them outside of us through our projection, we judge and either attack or attempt to avoid them. We feel attacked just by their presence and are sometimes literally attacked by them. Our shadow figures inside are like anchors that hold us back from going forward. The ego uses them to cover darker shadows but all of this in the final analysis is used by the ego to hide our true goodness, innocence, love and power. Specifically the ego uses a shadow to cover a gateway in the mind, which is a place of initiation that raises our consciousness. These gateways connect us to parts of the mind that have been lost or cut off from us. Since we tend to shy away from the parts of our minds that have shadows, the ego uses the shadows to hide the gateways. The shadows in our mind aren't solid but more like 3-D projections and the gateway is hidden inside the shadow.

In our dreams the 'monsters' and 'bad guys' that chase us are really just our shadow figures wanting to come home, to be forgiven and reintegrated. If we forgive a person on the outside, who represents a shadow figure for us, it has the healing effect of self-forgiveness and integration of the shadow figure on the inside. This turns all of the negative shadow energy into positive energy within us with an antidote against future negativity from this kind of shadow. Having forgiven and integrated the shadow on the inside, we no longer judge or project onto those outside us. This allows us to see the other's innocence or hear the calls for help from those on to whom we would have otherwise projected our negative self-concepts.

Exercise

Who is a shadow figure in your life and what are the shadow qualities you can't stand?

Usually there are three styles that we act out when we have projected onto someone. The first is that we recognise we are doing the same thing as our shadow or, secondly, we hide and compensate for our shadow and feel like we'd rather die than ever do such a thing. We feel aghast or insulted that anyone could have ever thought that we are like our shadow figure. The third style is doing a little of both.

If we are compensating it will be difficult for us to identify at all with the shadow figure. What is helpful is to intuit when you judged and split off this piece of yourself.

Ask yourself:

If I were to know when I judged and split off this piece of myself, it was at the age of _____

If I were to know who was involved, it was probably

_____

If I were to know what occurred that I judged this part of myself, it was _____

Then ask yourself:

If I were to know what role or roles I played to compensate for this shadow it was probably _____

If I were to know how many of this type of shadow figure I have in this regard, it's probably _____

If I were to know how many roles I used to compensate for this it was probably _____

Now imagine that all these shadows are in front of you. Imagine them all melting into one big shadow figure. Now take all the roles and compensations you used to hide these shadow figures.

See them in front of you and melt them all into one big compensation.

Now melt the shadow figure and the compensation figure together. Embrace and melt what's left back into you. Stay quietly for a few moments with the feeling that results from this integration.

WAY 42 Outrigger Canoes

In Hawaii the canoes all have outriggers to navigate and survive the ocean without capsizing. In any other place than the water, these outriggers are both unwieldy and heavy. We have these same kinds of outriggers in relationships, because we are afraid of intimacy, and they hold us back. These relationship outriggers are many and varied, but one thing is sure, the number of outriggers a partner has is the same as the number of outriggers that we have. We may complain about theirs until we are blue in the face, but they will not change until we let go of ours first.

If we do not have a relationship, we sometimes have so many disabling outriggers that we can't even get our canoes into the water. We can spend our time complaining or attacking the opposite or same sex, but it does not help; it will not hide our outriggers or how unattractive they are in relationships. The following unappetising outriggers push partners away out of fear that may be obvious, or hidden: affairs, lack of emotional integrity (such as hysteria, neediness, independence and dissociation), superiority or inferiority, comparison, overwork or laziness, fusion with a family member, flirting and jealousy, holding on to an old relationship or to past memories, expectations, pornography and fantasy, control, roles, rules and duties, a win-lose attitude, addictions, indulgence,

compulsions, taboos, overuse of any form, demands,
sacrifice, aggression or withdrawal in sex, blame,
attack in communications, victim or victimiser
stances. These are all forms of outriggers that we use
to protect us from and in relationships. Actually many
'good' things can also be used as outriggers, such as
computers, phones, sports, TV, reading, studying,
hobbies, helping others, family, politics, work, business, busyness, childcare and many more. These outriggers generate both power struggle and deadness in
relationships.

The first thing about any complaint that we have
about anyone, especially a love partner, is that we
have something that is correspondingly just as bad.
This may be quite hidden, or it may be hidden only
to us. If we can first be honest with ourselves and
become aware of our corresponding behaviour or attitude, we can then take steps to change what is holding us back. There will then be a corresponding
behaviour change in this person or partner. This will
naturally occur unless we have been using this person
to hold ourselves back, in which case we need to
become honest with ourselves and move on. Anything
negative in anyone will generate an experience of suffering to the extent that we also have a corresponding negative issue inside of us. We can choose to be
at peace. We can choose to find the upsetting conflict
within us and forgive ourselves and them. We can
choose not to defend against any of the things we
want the most.

•

Exercise

It is time to make a close, honest examination of ourselves if we want to succeed. Do you have a major complaint with someone? Certainly there is some complaint about your partner, or a general complaint against men, women, bosses, hired help, etc. Use the strength of the complaint to know how strong the 'problem' is in you. We may have it very well disguised but it will affect us and those around us. We may be blind to our problem but it is glaring to those around us.

It is important to use what we see in others as an opportunity for self-awareness and healing. If not we tend to become blind, righteous, stubborn and complaining.

Once we find the 'problem' in ourselves we can ask our higher mind for help. Once we acknowledge our mistake, realise that there's surely a better way, which naturally includes more self-awareness and success, we can make the choice for change.

We could also integrate our outriggers into any compensations or disguises we have had for this behaviour and keep integrating all of this into our higher self until all layers are clear. This is simple. You just imagine the problem, the role that hid it and your higher mind all melting together. When this occurs, there will be peace within and willingness to join your partner or the person about whom you were complaining. Truly, the only way they'll get better is through your help, support, communication or self-healing. Anything other than this will become more of a fight. You may be righteous but you will suffer and it can only get worse with judgement and complaint.

WAY 43 Our Relationship to Others Shows Our Self-Concepts

Everyone around us is a reflection of one or more of our self-concepts. The world is a great mirror reflecting all of our self-concepts back to us. Our self-concepts are beliefs about ourselves, which generate perception and create our experience. All beliefs are, at one level, beliefs about ourselves. Anything negative we believe about something or someone else, we also believe about ourselves. We have literally tens of thousands of self-concepts within us. Each self-concept has its own logic system, so there can be many different ways of thinking within our own minds. This also means that there can be conflicts, not only about how an answer is attained, but also about what the answer is. Since all answers are meant to add to our happiness, each self-concept has its own idea of what that happiness is. Conflict is the result of two or more self-concepts each trying to reach their own goal of happiness. A conflict with another is an inner conflict projected outward.

Each self-concept arose as a result of the loss of the centre within us, which is full of grace, balance, light, peace, happiness, innocence, bonding and power. As each separation occurred and we lost bonding, self-concepts began to spring up. These self-concepts gave us illusions, which brought about mis-steps and pain.

Or they gave us sacrifice and the belief that we have to lose sometimes in order to succeed. We then try to dole out the sacrifice, so that we do not have all the burden ourselves, which either makes our partners less attractive or more combative.

We have even developed self-destructive or suicidal self-concepts that can be quite hidden from our conscious minds, but whose misunderstanding is so profound that they think that killing us would lead to peace, happiness or at least no more pain. I have seen numerous times, when a three-year-old 'self' inside thought that the best way to get us out of suffering was to die or be killed. Finally there are self-concepts that are in comas or even dead. These are self-concepts that were so overloaded by sacrifice or so overwhelmed by pain, that they became unconscious or died. Buried within us, these selves have a very negative effect on us and can be reflected in our world as others dying or in comas around us. Selves that died in us can later show up as miscarriages, stillbirths and abortions, to name a few aspects. These self-concepts can set up some very painful, traumatic events in our lives, which the ego will use to compound our buried pain and which our higher mind will use to try to alert us to the buried pain and dead 'selves' within us for healing. The negative 'selves' can generate heartbreak and tragedy in our lives.

One way to heal and even prevent these types of problems is to dissolve the self-concepts as we discover them. This dissolution can be done in many ways, such as letting go or making another choice as we discover the self-concepts involved. Forgiveness, integration, finding the gifts or deeper self-concepts that the more shallow self-concepts hide are a few ways to heal or let go of self-concepts.

Typically, as we go through life we build up our self-concepts until we have a strong ego. In doing this we become very independent and dissociate most of our needy, painful or guilty self-concepts, building compensating self-concepts that are strong, independent, 'demanding', perfectionist, distracted, attached, hard working, busy, overwhelmed, controlling, dutiful, caught in roles and sacrificing.

To progress from this point we must begin to heal ourselves, learn partnership and interdependence and begin to let go of these self-concepts. Each self-concept gives us a job and doesn't allow us to enjoy ourselves in life, except momentarily as we complete our jobs. As we let go of our negative beliefs about ourselves, especially shadow figures or concepts of self-hatred, we stop attacking or punishing ourselves so much. When we integrate the negative and the compensating self-concepts that hide them, we achieve a new level of confidence, integrated goals and ability to receive, ending as well a conflict or potential conflict in our world. As we heal we give up the separation and boundaries of the ego for love and grace and an authentic sense of 'we' built on a true and centred 'I'. As we progress and evolve there becomes less of the 'I' and more of heaven.

Every self-concept gives us a job. This is where our 'doing' comes from. Once we lose bonding and our 'being', the 'doing' of self-concepts spring up. Our being is who we are at our centre, a child of God.

Our jobs give us a sense of what we have to do. So, typically, we evolve and grow in our becoming. Our becoming leads us closer and closer to our beingness, until we can eventually spend most of our time in a state of being. This allows us effectiveness, happiness and love without necessarily having to do anything. Our being is a place without thinking, a place of no-mindedness – a place of sensual aliveness, because we are not busy thinking or doing. Our centre is a place of peace, humour and joy where as a question or problem arises the answer appears simultaneously.

Our minds are crammed with self-concepts all vying for attention, all wanting to run the show except, of course, for the depressed selves who have not got over certain losses, the burnt-out selves who came about through overwork or emotional overload, the unconscious or dead selves who were overwhelmed in the course of directing our lives. Healing or letting go of these self-concepts allows us to jettison stress and feel free. As we let go of more and more of these self-concepts, we stop living life through recipes and enjoy more spontaneity and creativity.

Usually we have our 'nice', 'good', 'hardworking' self-concepts hiding our negative self-concepts. These in turn hide our most hated self-concepts, which in turn hide our true identity as a child of God, deserving every ease, grace and abundance.

Exercise

Take a pen and paper or a tape recorder or get someone to help you. Ask yourself, or get someone to ask you:

What does this negative situation prove about you? ___
_____

Whatever 'pops' into your mind, which is always the best way to do this exercise, is your self-concept.

After you have started this exercise, say to yourself or have your friend ask:

The self-concepts that these self-concepts hide are _____
_____

As you keep asking this question, you will typically go through the many layers of self-concepts in the mind, sometimes alternating from negative and positive ones into the very dark, negative ones and finally into the very positive ones. You may want to go a little farther when you hit the first positive ones because many times there are further caches of negative beliefs about yourself based under them.

Sometimes you may not have something pop into your mind, but the feeling or emotion you are having is the answer to the question. Just say the feeling and keep on going. Sometimes 'I don't know' pops into your head. It is an 'I don't know' self concept. Just use that as the answer and continue to ask the question, 'The self-concepts these hide are. . .?'. Usually it's easy-going in this exercise but sometimes it is not straightforward. In these circumstances, however, it can be all the more valuable. Sometimes it can take only ten minutes or go over an hour. Keep going until you hit a state of high joy.

In fact, any situation in the world or your life can be used to start this exercise, but for the sake of our present focus, use the person with whom you're having the biggest or most chronic issue. Just ask yourself:

The self-concept that this person or situation proves about me is _____

As you begin from the self-concepts that emerge as you ask the question about what self-concept this problem relationship reflects about you, a great many more will emerge. As you begin and each self-concept shows itself, merely keep asking the same question successively until you reach feelings of freedom and bliss for at least a couple of minutes.

Just keep asking the question:

> *This self-concept hides the self-concept of* _____
> *or*
> *This hides* _____

You'll notice that as you come up with each new self-concept, the old one fades away because at one level it was just a defence to hide a deeper self-concept. You'll notice that you will repeat certain self-concepts. As you repeat certain self-concepts, each succeeding time it is a much deeper self-concept. If you examine your feelings, you will notice that the latter one is much deeper.

   Following this exercise, I have asked people to intuit the amount of time that the released self-concepts have demanded in terms of work and pain. Some people have reported that they felt that they had saved hundreds and even thousands of years of what would have been negativity, darkness and a great deal of suffering in their lives.

WAY 44 Karmic Stories

'Karma' means 'action' in Sanskrit. A karmic story is a story of the mind that sets a pattern in our lives. This is a fascinating aspect of an area of the mind that I call the unconscious or 'soul' mind. In this mind there are stories filled with all kinds of issues. Many people label these stories as 'other lifetimes', while others consider them to be just the same sort of mind fabrication we have in dreams. It is the depiction of issues made into a story to describe the soul's development in metaphoric terms. Whether you call these stories 'other lifetimes' or metaphors, they exist.

Healing the levels of pain and negative stories that exist on this level of the mind can have a dramatic and positive effect on our lives. I had my first experience of this in a therapeutic setting over twenty-five years ago and have had many thousands of experiences of working at this level of the mind ever since. My first experiences were so dramatic and transforming for the individuals involved that I tended to glamorise this area of the mind. But as I moved past the psychic, shamanic mind to the spiritual area of the mind, it became just another of the fascinating areas of the mind that presented itself for healing. Whether you believe in 'other lifetimes' or consider these all to be fanciful stories, they depict patterns in the mind that need healing. Sometimes these karmic stories are the easiest ways that our minds can represent what it is inside us that needs healing.

One dramatic story concerns a middle-aged man who came to me for some sessions in 1979 to heal the relationship with his hated mother-in-law.

This man went through some preliminary sessions in which we worked with the healing principles of forgiveness and integration. Yet for some reason we weren't making much headway in the sense that there was little change in my client's feelings toward his 'hated' mother-in-law. Finally, I decided to heal the family roots carried over to his issue with his mother-in-law. I asked him if the problem began before, during or after his birth, he replied, 'Before. Way before. I'm seeing a scene where I'm a peasant and there's going to be a hunt. Except I'm what is going to be hunted. I'm given an hour's start and then dogs and men on horses are tracking me. Finally, I'm caught by the dogs and torn apart. Now I see another scene where I'm in charge and having her put to death. Now I see another scene where she is poisoning me. Now I see a scene where I am choking her to death . . .'

He kept breathlessly relating scene after scene. Finally, realising that it would take a couple of hours to process all of these 'karmic stories', I asked him to go to the root life story where the conflict began with the two of them. He then began to describe a life in the middle ages where as a man he had been in a major conflict inside himself, which he labelled as the conservative, reactionary side of himself versus the liberal, progressive side. He was in so much torment because of that conflict that he described his soul splitting apart in the next life and coming in as two different people still in a fight, with him becoming the more progressive side.

I had heard many strange things in therapy before, but this was the strangest thing I had heard to date. I simply used the metaphors he presented, then proceeded to go back to the original 'life' or 'story' as you prefer and helped him to integrate those two conflicting aspects of himself in a simple integration exercise. Once that was accomplished, I asked him to bring the resolution and good feeling of that life, which in his imagination had now turned out successfully, up through all of his other lives until the present. As he did this, the expression on his face changed from intently serious to radiantly smiling. He felt jubilant as he left that day and when he returned the next week he reported that his mother-in-law had seemed to change overnight and that they were quickly building a friendship, were no longer offended by each others' humour and were actually carrying on together in great fun.

With this client I had simply used the metaphor he presented to me and joined it to healing exercises the way I would have with a dream or a story from childhood. Yet this was enough to have a dramatic effect on his relationship with his mother-in-law and change the very tenor and quality of his life.

Exercise

I will present two different healing exercises for the 'karmic story' or the 'other lifetime'. Use whichever one you prefer.

You can use this exercise to see what your mind presents in regard to healing with a certain person. It may present nothing. Trust that, but you can use these exercises for any healing situation to check if there are unconscious underpinnings.

Karmic Story

Ask yourself these questions, using your intuition to answer. If you find yourself thinking rather than guessing, it is your ego's way of stopping you. Here is the story metaphor exercise:

If I were to know if I have any stories regarding this person, situation, or experience, they are probably _____

_____

If I were to know what that story is, it's probably ____

_____

If I were to know what character I am in this story, it's probably _____

If I were to know what character this other person is in this story, if any, it's probably _____

If I were to know what dark lesson I learned in this story it was probably _____

If I were to know the light lesson or the lesson God wanted me to learn in this story, it's probably _____

If I were to know the gift hiding under this dark story, against which this story is a defence, it's probably

_____

Go back to the very beginning of the story and see yourself embracing God's lesson and the gift that awaits you.

When you feel the gift and the lesson inside you, go back through the story to see and feel how it turns out now. If it's not 100 percent better, there is probably another gift awaiting you there as well.

Other Lifetime Story
Ask yourself intuitively:

If I were to know in what lifetime this karmic story began, it was one that I lived in the country that's now called _____

If I were to know if I was a man or a woman, I was probably a _____

If I were to know who I knew in that lifetime that I know in this one, it's probably _____

If there was someone, ask:

If I were to know what relationship they were in with me, it was probably _____

If I were to know what occurred there, it was probably

_____

If I were to know what lesson I came to learn in that life, it was probably _____

If I were to know what gift I had come to give in that lifetime, learning that lesson and giving that gift, it was probably _____

If I were to know how well I succeeded in that lifetime, it was probably _____

Now go back to the very beginning of that life and embrace the lesson you had come to learn and the gift you had come to give.

Bring the energy of that gift and lesson all the way

through that life sharing them with everyone and every-thing.

How does that life turn out now?

Bring the energy of that now successful life into and through every life you and this 'problem' person need for it to heal the roots of your relationship now. Bring it through this life up until the present moment. . .

How does that feel? If it doesn't feel great, there is another root lifetime that must be healed. Just repeat the exercise aiming for that lifetime.

WAY 45 Any Conflict is Really a Fear of Having It All

About ten years ago, after more than twenty years as a therapist, I began to discover something very interesting happening when we pierced down into the primordial dynamics of people's problems. Many times we would reach a bottom line level where people were creating difficulty because they were afraid to have it all. They would voice different aspects of this fear, such as: 'If I have it all and things are good, then I'll disappear or die', or 'I'll go into meltdown and lose my identity in the Oneness', or 'If I had it all, what would my family and friends think?' or 'I can't have it all while so many people are suffering'.

Many people share a common fear that if they are really happy they will lose control. The fear that under-lies all of the other guilts and fears is not fear of death, as one might imagine, but the fear of life being that good. Somehow the very notion of it makes people uncomfortable, even though it is for what they are consciously striving.

A good definition of a conflict or an area in which we cannot succeed is one the conscious mind wants and works hard for but one the deeper mind rejects out of guilt or fear.

Each problem is a crossroads. It is a choice either to receive a gift or to keep the problem. The gift is a

> What you need
> You will urgently seek
>   Yet secretly push away.
>
>   Chuck Spezzano, *Awaken the Gods*

chance to step forward in consciousness, while the problem actually slows down the unfolding process and gives us a modicum of control. I have learned that one of the easiest ways to resolve conflict, no matter how dire it seems, is to receive the gift that life is offering you.

Exercise

Today, begin to examine how you might be using this conflict with others to hold yourself back from something good. Ask yourself what this might be. If it does not immediately present itself, dwell on it. Let it be a question you reflect on directly and indirectly until you are willing to have the answer. At a subconscious level, you have in your life only those things you are not afraid to have. You could use this principle to re-examine what you say you want in your life and what you actually have. So, despite complaints to the contrary, we have only what we are not afraid to have.

Once you have guessed what good thing you might be frightened to have in your life, ask yourself intuitively what frightens you about having this good thing. The answers that come forth pop right out of the subconscious mind. Explore this area as much as you can on your own and then with your partner. If you experience resistance to this concept, do not believe it, but pretend it was true, and examine it yourself and with your partner to see what you might turn up. It is this that can provide a whole other perspective on your problems.

WAY 46 Vampires and Toxic People

We all have deeply buried self-concepts or person-alities in which we have a belief that we are poisonous. It is a place where we believe that situations or people go wrong because of us. As a result of this belief about ourselves we unconsciously push people away from us, even people we love a great deal.

'Vampires' and 'toxic people' are shadow figures. They are places of self-hatred that we bury within us and sometimes act out. Vampires are people who emotionally or psychically suck the energy from others. They are 'takers' who at times go to an unusual degree of taking from others. They are typically blind to their behaviour and demand attention, support and energy, and they have no idea why people, even their own children, avoid them like the plague. Vampires are typically people who have been victimised and taken from by others and feel justified in the way they are acting. This righteousness alienates those around them and stops many avenues of help coming to them.

Toxic men or toxic women have become that way by experiences that left them bitter. They also feel justified in their negative behaviour and in doing what they do regardless of its effect on those around them. They don't realise that they have a bad attitude and can literally dominate a situation in a very negative way by their presence, to the point where it sours the situation for everyone present. Toxic people can be negative, domineering, authoritarian, belligerent, bullying, obstreperous, demanding and hateful. Their unawareness of their own process leads them to be righteous and cantankerous.

If we do not heal this problem of the toxic or vampire shadow as reflected by a person around us, we will not only feel victimised, we will also catch or inherit their problem. Then we will act out this same behaviour later with just as negative a result or we will bury it and compensate for it, becoming a vampire or toxic person magnet. If we have people in our environments that are that destructive, it will take total dedication on our parts to get along with them. It is not by accident but by design that we are in this situation. If we succeed, it can springboard us forward in life, giving us a whole new level of confidence and success. First, however, we must realise that the toxic or vampire-like people around us reflect self-concepts in our own minds. It is an opportunity to heal these negative, self-attacking beliefs within while having a mirror outside us to know how well we are doing with our healing. If one of our parents acted this way, it means that we came to heal this deep-seated soul fragment as acted out by others around us caught in this same trap.

Exercise

As you commit to find and heal those shadow parts of vampires and toxic people there are a couple of strategies that can help. First ask yourself what they must be feeling to act the way they are acting, since we act the way we do because of how we're feeling.

Secondly, every time you think of them, feel and see a bridge of light connecting from the light of your spirit to the light of theirs.

Every time you see them, look past their body to the part within that is wounded and causing the upset. Pour your love and ask heaven's help to pour love to the wounded parts, many of which are 'selves' emotionally arrested when they were children. When these parts receive enough love they will grow up to the problem person's present age and melt back into them, reconnecting some of the wires that were cut inside their hearts and minds.

You are never in a situation that can't be healed by giving. What is it you are called to give in this situation to make it better?

Commit to the person reflecting a shadow figure as being on your team. Commit to them as your friend. Keep a log for yourself about any improvements you see in them, your attitude toward them, how they behave and your relationship with them. Acknowledge and compliment them for any forward progress.

In any situation where there is a problem, you have a gift that will transform it. Go to that place in your mind where your gifts are kept in potential. Open the door to your gift and embrace it. What is it? Now imagine yourself sharing it with this person and it will increase for you as it helps them. What does heaven want to pass through you for them? Receive that and share it with them as well. Repeat this exercise with anyone from the past who was toxic or vampire-like until they are free.

If the negative experience with this person is happening

at this time in your life, you have probably transferred it from an earlier experience that you had with a toxic person. There is a good chance that if this is true, then part of your purpose has to do with being able to help people like this. Helping is a lot better than running from these people and suffering when you can't. Ask for the grace to learn what you've come to learn about healing vampires or toxic people.

Forgive them and yourself.

Ask yourself:

If I were to know where this root began in me, if it was before, during or after my birth, it was probably _____

_____

If it was before your birth ask that if this experience took place in the womb or before that, it was probably

_____

If it was before your experience in the womb ask:

If it was something passed down through the family or another lifetime or a challenge my soul brought in to heal so it would have a gift for the world, it's probably_____

_____

If it is an ancestral pattern go to the exercise from the 'Healing Negative Stories' chapter (see page 147).

If it is 'another' life story go to the exercise from the 'Karmic Stories' chapter (see page 170).

If it is a challenge brought in by your soul to learn and grow ask for the lesson, gifts, and grace to come to you now so it can be accomplished.

If the root experience took place in the womb ask:

If I was to know which month it began in, it was probably in the _____ month.

Then continue with questions asking who was present, etc.

If it was after birth ask:

If I were to know how old I was when this problem began, it was probably at the age of _____

If I were to know who was present, it was probably

_____

If I were to know what was occurring, it was probably

_____

If I were to know how this scene affected me and what I began to believe afterwards as a result, it was probably

_____

Now choose what you would believe instead of the negative choices you made.

Go to the place inside that carries your gifts. What did you bring in as gifts to help yourself and everyone in this situation? Open the door to all these gifts.

First embrace the gift you brought for yourself.

Now embrace the gifts you brought in for everyone in this scene.

Share the gifts you brought in for each person.

Then receive the gift that heaven has for you and then the gifts that heaven has for each of the people in the scene.

Now as heaven's gift comes through you, share it with them.

Now as the scene resolves itself, receive the gifts that they have for you.

Now receive the gifts that heaven wants to pass through them for you.

If the scene that popped in was as an adult or teenager, there's a good chance that at least one more important incident happened in childhood with an even deeper root going all the way back into the womb.

Take your time but do this exercise until you reach an experience at least back in the womb. This will clear out a great deal if not all of the problem.

Ask yourself how many layers of integration, if you were to know, would need to occur to show a marked difference in your problem person. This would reflect how many layers of conflicts in your mind need to be healed within yourself to have the person who is your mirror begin to change. Now ask your higher mind to accomplish all of the integrations needed for there to be a marked improvement in your problem person.

Ask yourself:

If I were to know how many vampire shadow figures I have, it's about _____

If I were to know how many compensations I use to hide this shadow, it would probably be _____

Now see all the vampire shadows in front of you along with all the compensations. Melt the vampires and all their compensations together and when that is complete melt it all back into you.

Do this now with the toxic people shadow figures.

Ask yourself:

If I were to know how many toxic people shadows I have inside, it's probably _____

See them all standing in front of you. Melt them into one big toxic person.

Recognise it as a hologram, a three dimensional projection that isn't solid. The ego uses shadows to hide gateways in your mind. These gateways are places of initiation. As you step into the shadow figure, see the gateway and go through it, you step into a part of your mind that's been lost to you. In the rare cases this part of the mind is dark or scary, ask your higher mind to do the house cleaning and lightening of this area for you.

Ask yourself intuitively what percentage of your mind you just regained. However much you regained will give you that much more mind power.

Repeat this exercise with any vampire shadows you still have.

Ask for a miracle for yourself and this 'negative' person and the situation you are in every day.

WAY 47 Indulgence or Relationship?

When we have a relationship or something in our relationship that seems to obstruct us, it points to hidden or not-so-hidden indulgence in our lives. While we use indulgence as a way of rewarding ourselves for achievement, it is really a compensation for sacrifice. Just as an obstruction points to indulgence, an indulgence points to sacrifice as a compensating balance. Indulgence is something we take but do not receive. It does not refresh us, it burns us out and exhausts us as much as sacrifice. The hangover we have from our indulgence is something from which we need to rest, just as much as from our sacrifice. Like sacrifice, indulgence uses us up, wears us out and affects our health. With sacrifice and indulgence, we can't receive. Indulgence does not relieve or renew us, but makes us emptier. If the cycle of indulgence-sacrifice is maintained, it leads to exhaustion, feelings of valuelessness and meaninglessness.

The degree of problem either in our relationship, or with another relationship, speaks of how much hidden indulgence we have going on in our lives. Both indulgence and sacrifice stop levels of joining and relatedness, which is what makes a relationship successful. Indulging in all the little goodies we want to get for ourselves, which we think will satisfy us, never succeeds in making us happy. We are trying to get a level of comfort or fulfilment that can only come from love, friendship and relatedness. Only these are satisfying, fulfilling and rejuvenating. Indulgence and sacrifice, which come from broken bonding, old pain and levels of separation, create a 'me-first' or 'me-only' selfish attitude. We are then too soft or too hard on ourselves, depending on whether we are in the indulgent or sacrifice side of the cycle. Either extreme behaviours or combinations of the two promote self-attack and are harmful to relationships in that they stop intimacy and block equality.

It is time to realise what truly satisfies us and to be willing to change if we've been on the wrong track. Even if we have lived our whole lives in a way that hasn't worked, it is crucial to realise this about our lives. It's now time to learn what will truly bring success. We all have to start someplace. The sooner we examine what isn't working, or what we aren't receiving, and realise that it's something for which we're responsible, the sooner we can make new decisions to change.

Hopefully, we will all have this wake-up call in our lives, either all at once or gradually over time, and mature as a result. Every little indulgence in our lives is filling a place in our minds where bonding and joy belong. Let us have the courage to let go of our indulgences today, so we can have that which really makes us happy. If we don't feel we have the courage, it is at least important to ask our higher mind to demonstrate, as easily as possible, what effect the indulgence is having on our lives and what the effect of true connection would do for us. This would motivate us to make the choice for change. Every obstruction that stops us from getting what we want points to something that we are trying to get outside ourselves. When obstructed, the ego always suggests attack, which will sooner or later lead to suffering. Only our choice for peace will work and only what we give will succeed to make the situation better.

Exercise

Examine the obstruction in your present relationship or the obstructing relationship. The next step is to look for the corresponding indulgence. This is easier than it seems because conflict hides indulgence. If you have trouble working out a particular indulgence, try to see it intuitively (ask yourself and accept the first answer that comes to your mind). Study this indulgence. What loss is it trying to make up for? Has it made you happy? Ever? What would it take for you to let go of it?

Keep dwelling on the present indulgence, studying its effect on your life. Now look for the corresponding feeling of sacrifice. Sometimes a person experiences this sacrifice as a feeling that depresses or exhausts them and they do not get much done. On the other hand, some people just cannot do enough as a compensation. At some point reason will show you you've been getting a bad deal. It is at this point that you can choose to let go of your indulgence for the gifts that await you. Hiding behind every indulgence is a gift, which will truly satisfy you. Knowing this can make it easier to let go of our indulgence for the truth of what would make us happy.

If there is some part in your relationship where you are

not joining in intimacy and success, then there is an indul-
gence that is more cherished and a corresponding sacri-
fice in the way. Choose to find it and let it go. There's got
to be a better way.

If there is someone you are fighting, if only in your
mind, it again speaks of a trap of indulgence that you
hide, pretend to know nothing about or make a 'good'
excuse for because of some circumstance in your life. Choose
to find it and let it go. There's got to be a better way.

WAY 48 The Plan of the Ego

The ego's plan is to rule and to be special. The ego is the principle of separation and it uses every negative emotion to establish itself and make itself stronger. The ego uses every painful incident that could be used for release and freedom to compound the pain and to bring about a dark lesson to increase the negative beliefs and painful perception we have about life. It promises to help us stop the fear, but only some of it, because the ego is made up of fear, pain and guilt; it is only interested in stopgap measures. For the most part it is invested in keeping the status quo. It therefore suggests we 'adjust' to situations rather than transform them, and it suggests compromise where both parties then feel like they have lost and no real joining or change occurs. One of the best ways to keep us from evolving is to keep us in power struggle and competition.

Another ego ploy is to keep us in judgement and grievances, which generate problems that obstruct and delay us, shutting and closing off our minds to inspiration and grace. Judgement and grievance are generated from our hidden guilt, which leads to stubbornness, and feelings of failure. This leads to the kind of compensating righteousness and idealism that is willing to kill people or judge them as deserving of hell for political or religious differences. The ego wants to be indispensable to us so it can continue its existence. It makes a pact with us, telling us it will take care of us and handle everything, if only we do not bother questioning and just follow its guidance. We spend the first part of our lives building up our egos to get along in the world, and if we keep growing and evolving we need to begin dismantling and melting away the ego to open ourselves further, to be able to give, receive, love and feel joy. This allows us to experience happiness at greater levels and go on to experience more grace and higher levels of consciousness.

Our ego encourages us to identify with our bodies as our selves. This means we will both believe in death and fear it. It also then tells us our bodies are not good enough for us and attacks us endlessly about it.

It consistently makes up strategies that it convinces us are for our own good and happiness. These strategies work at times, but they never bring us happiness. They only succeed in building up the ego. It entrenches us in conflict, victim-victimiser roles, sacrifice and untrue helping roles, which look good but are only compensations. It continuously attacks and criticises us under the guise of improving us. Its entire goal is to hamper and obstruct us in the guise of helping us. It wants to distract and delay us from what really works and what would melt it away bit by bit.

Finally the ego gets us into what seems like an unliveable and impossible place in life. Here it suggests that we lay down and die rather than find the way out of the death conspiracy to a new vision in our lives. When our ego is telling us it's time to die, life is actually giving us an invitation to rebirth. These situations are proof of the ego's insanity, for it believes it will continue beyond our death. So it attempts to engineer our death and then somehow live beyond us. This is like the cartoon characters of our youth that were always sawing off branches high up in a tree from a position on the end of the branch.

The alternative to listening to the ego mind is to follow the direction of our higher minds. This part of our minds is gifted with reason, creativity, inspiration, vision, being, peace and grace. It contains all of our answers and it's the part of us that connects with the universal mind and Oneness. As we begin to learn the difference in our two minds and listen more to the guidance of our higher minds, we become more and more successful. The ego's voice is urgent, loud, demanding and distracting, while the higher mind's voice is quiet, suggesting ways that everyone can win now and for always. The ego always recommends a way for itself to win either in the long or short run. The ego wants to dominate and, if it cannot win the competition, it wants to become special in some way, even by major painful loss. The ego always wants glamour and attention for itself, always doing everything by itself, and wanting people and things around to demonstrate how special it is, attacking those who don't but reserving the most lethal levels of self-attack for ourselves.

The higher mind works for love, partnership, intimacy, shared success, mutuality, uniqueness, fulfilment, living our purpose, embracing our destinies, knowing our true identities as spirit and thus being nobody special in its own eyes, but embracing its greatness as a child of God.

The ego's plan is to prove that others did it wrong, that God did it wrong, and that it should then rule the universe. The ego is not above generating a great deal of pain and loss for itself to show that God failed, and it should be in charge of the universe. The ego is not above generating disaster and tragedy for us to show that it should be in charge, to rebel or get revenge.

We always have the choice about which mind we will listen to. This choice determines our experience as either healing and joyful or the ego's proof that we were right all the time, that we are the most special one, and that we should be in charge. The ego's plan contains the strategies of getting, taking, excuses, justification, proving, compensating, revenge, heartbreak, illness, accidents, loss, domination, slavery, holding on, control, valuelessness, failure, conspiracies, inadequacy, inability to commit, perfectionism, demands, expectations, sacrifice, roles, dark stories, hiding, inauthenticity, giving to take, any way to call attention to itself, glamour, idols, shadows or specialness.

The plan of the ego imprisons us and keeps us small. It blocks what truly brings joy and fulfilment, such as love, creativity, grace, living our purpose, joining, giving, receiving, helpfulness, ease and humour. It suggests indulgence, glamour, adrenaline, competitiveness, sacrifice, hardship, self-attack, separation, neediness and unrequitedness. It is time to put our lives in order. If our egos had been a financial advisor, it would have led us to bankruptcy, ruthless winning or dishonesty. But it would not show us the way to worry-free abundance.

Not getting along with someone, rather than finding a mutual solution or a healing, falls right into the ego's plan for distraction and delays. The ego does everything in its power to block mutuality, progress and love. This person who is a problem for us is vital to show us a hidden, rejected 'self' that is in conflict within, eating away at us. When we heal the conflict within, we will only feel gratitude toward the person for helping us find what was too hidden to find, yet too harmful to ignore.

Exercise

Take a good look at the scarcity and lack of receiving in your life. Examine what has been dull, boring and stuck in your life. Examine your neediness and lack of response to your emotional or sexual needs. Observe the times you have been a victim or a victimiser. Reflect on the times you have lorded it over, dominated or grovelled and been subservient to others. Observe your need to win and your competitiveness, and the times you lost and failed. Take a close look at your accidents, illness, indulgences and addictions, along with the things and people you thought would save you and make you happy, and with whom you were disillusioned.

Consider your lack of satisfaction regarding your relationships. Any place where there's been a lack of success, there's been an ego strategy at work. Examine if you want to keep going down the ego's path. Examine if the ego has kept its promises to you and you are happy. If you are not, it's time to change your allegiance, commit to your higher mind and listen to its guidance. Realise that if everyone doesn't get to win equally, the ego has inveigled its way into your allegiance again. The higher mind always has an answer that allows for your own and everyone's success. It will move you forward, sometimes by leaps and bounds. Sit quietly today and listen to its suggestion for the answer to the problem of getting along with someone. It will give you the answer as soon as your willingness to have it is stronger than your fear. If somehow you are too frightened, remember that change will only lead to greater success and your higher mind will always help you by increasing your willingness.

Not getting along with someone is just part of the ego's plan to delay and distract you from the solution and the gift that is the reward for the resolution. Take some quiet time today to sit and listen for the answer.

WAY 49 Getting Along with God

A little over two years ago, when I had been counselling and coaching for twenty-eight years, I began to discover a whole level of the mind that I never suspected. While the first inklings began over five years ago, it wasn't until three years later that everything crystallised. I finally realised that there was an area of the mind that was the deepest aspect yet to show up in the pre-enlightened states of the mind.

Let me review for a moment a model of understanding that I have frequently used to help people transform problems. One of the best aspects of this model is that it is practical, and it can help people out of pain. The model begins with the *conscious* mind. The conscious mind is that of which we are aware. This is like the tip of an iceberg, and it is actually the smallest part of the mind. Next there is the *subconscious*, what we consciously hide from ourselves. This is everything that has occurred from conception and shows that we have forgotten more than we remember in our lives. The subconscious mind includes our family dynamics, and some of our shadow figures, buried aggression, sexuality and threatening emotions and life experiences, which set up both our relationship and life patterns for success or failure.

Deeper than our family patterns are our soul

patterns or the *unconscious* mind. This part contains vision, ancestral patterns, archetypes, shadow figures, dark healing stories, conspiracies, our purpose, idols of attachment, soul-level gifts, valuelessness, our destiny, past-life metaphors, deep-seated painful emotions, shamanic consciousness and mastery.

Finally, there are the spiritual aspects and issues of our mind. We could call this our *superconscious*. It contains our higher mind, which connects our soul mind and spirit, which is the creative channel of God's love and grace. This part also contains our relationship to God or however we conceive our higher power. It also contains our resistance to all things spiritual along with our idols, or those things, people or situations that we thought would save us and make us happy. We have tried to make other things (such as money, sex or fame) into God and finally these become our gods. This area of the mind contains meaninglessness, the battleground between heaven's meaning and our ego. It reflects our relationship to God, love, Oneness and it contains the shadow figure of the rebel.

Our relationship with God also shows the root and most important patterns of the mind in terms of getting along with absolutely anyone. The relationship we have with anyone is a reflection of our primordial relationship with God. Everything we feel or think about anyone else, we feel and think about God. As we improve our relationship with God we also then improve our relationship with everyone else. Let me give an example that occurred recently. Someone was complaining about a business relationship saying that he didn't feel included in the partnership and that he felt both used and abandoned by an ex-partner. He felt that he was in sacrifice the whole time he had worked with his ex-partner, who he felt had not really acted like a true partner. Even at the point when the partnership was breaking up, the ex-partner admitted to rebellion and getting revenge on him, out of jealousy for his position. I asked him to whom he intuitively thought he might be doing the same thing. He replied, 'God.' I asked if he felt excluded, used, abandoned and made to sacrifice by God. He replied that upon consideration, he actually did feel all of those feelings about God.

I then said, 'Well, if God actually didn't include you, you'd wink out of existence. You would not even be. As a result of that, God, no longer acting as the highest principle of love, light and power in the universe, would stop being God and everything would wink out of existence. If God didn't include us or did anything else that we blamed him for doing then he'd lose his God licence and we'd all be in trouble.' I went on to say, 'If God did any of these things, God couldn't stay God. This would then give us the excuse to take over as God since God was making such a muddle of things. For evidence that we should be God we need only look at the world to prove that God is derelict and as our ego has been saying all along, we should be God! Of course, if God is responsible or guilty for the world or any of the things we are accusing him of doing, then God stops being God, the principle of love and giving all to all, and everything falls apart because God has lost his God franchise. In the deepest most hidden part of the mind we see the evidence that anything we hold against anyone we hold against God.'

God, of course, can't fail in any way, by definition, but we could blame him for all of our failures and project onto him everything we are doing and use it as our excuse to take over.

I then asked the businessman if he could see that he was using this situation to rebel and get revenge on God out of jealousy.

He replied, 'Yes, of course.'

I asked if he'd be willing to forgive God for what he'd been doing.

He said 'Of course!'

I then asked if he'd let go of this mistaken strategy, so he could just be a child of God rather than to try to be God.

He said, 'Sure.'

I then asked how he felt about his ex-partner.

He replied, 'I feel fine. I feel happy.'

This man had obviously done a lot of work on himself to be able to uncover this deepest level of the mind so easily. Once we heal this level of the mind we can enjoy our mastery, innocence, power and radiating love. This area is not easily uncovered unless we know about it. Once we access an awareness of this level of the mind, we find an easy way to transform a chronic relationship or a layer of what needs to be healed.

Exercise

Take a relationship that is troubling you. What are the mistakes you think this person is making?

Do you think that God is doing the same thing to you that the person with whom you're having trouble is doing? This may sound preposterous at first, but spend sometime reflecting on it.

Of course, you realise God couldn't do any of these negative things or fail to do what is positive and still remain God.

So if you think God has been doing this to you, do you think it might be possible that you were the one doing all of these things and blaming God for it?

Would you forgive God for what you've been doing?

Would you forgive yourself for this mistake?

Would you let go of trying to be God and let yourself be a child of God, deserving ease, a beautiful life and every good thing?

Relax and let go. Let God run the show. We push ourselves too much to find the answers to our quest for happiness and successful relationships when the answers are there all the time.

WAY 50 Rebellion or Destiny?

All of us have a destiny that is so powerful and beautiful that most of us feel it is too much, too frightening or too special. We turn away from both our destinies and ourselves. We turn away from heaven. We rebel against what wants to be given to us. We have forgotten who we are and we rebel against the power of our genius and reduce it to resisting and creative hiding, like everyone else in the crowd. In our effort to be included, we betray ourselves. This does not bring us inclusion; it merely allows us to be alone together with everyone else. It will never satisfy our need for joining, which can and will eventually bring us all the way to Oneness, something that our ego fights.

We attack authority whether it shows itself in others, ourselves or God. We become frightened of power and seek indulgence rather than joy. We run from ourselves, guaranteeing deep-seated feelings of failure that we hide by sacrifice in an effort to compensate. Our mind has become split and who we are is lost to us. This guarantees that we cannot succeed or be deeply happy. We learn to adjust and settle, pretending we never had a chance. This affords us, at best, only momentary glimpses of happiness and peace. We are on the wrong path by design, proving that we won't be forced into anything, but in truth avoiding the only path that would grant us freedom. We have fallen into the unenviable position of being afraid not only of our freedom, but also of ourselves. Only with a deep willingness and desire to be open to the truth and grace, can we remember who we are. Only in this way can we find ourselves once again.

The path of destiny is a path of compassion and genius. There are rare, visionary gifts within us that would help free humanity. These gifts are so exquisitely stunning that their beauty can leave us breathless. These gifts are an act of trust and willingness to find the way within us, to give a gift of love to humanity, to ourselves and to God.

To embrace our destiny is to help find the way home for everyone in a world where most seek to lose themselves in distractions. The need for specialness has become the primary focus in a world where so many have lost their way. Specialness is the demand that others treat us as the most important one, meeting our needs first. Our need for specialness hides our greatness and our purpose, which is unique and special to us. It is the contribution we can make to help the world. Our destiny recognises that we have come to know our place on earth and in heaven. It recognises our identity as a child of God, deserving every good thing and all abundance. It carries the surety of faith with a deep abiding peace that smiles at most illusions. As we embrace our destiny we realise that we are only upset to the extent that we let ourselves be, no matter what the circumstance.

Not getting along with others is merely one of the common ways in which we hide. We get so caught up in those who are a problem to us that we obsess about it. We get caught in fighting and righteousness, seeing only our own point of view, wasting endless amounts of time arguing with people in our head, both past and present. By not forgiving where another seems to obstruct us, we are left to judgement, which shrinks our mind and its ability to envision possibilities and solutions. When we judge we rob ourselves of inspiration, peace, love and joy and when we judge others, it is then that they are in most need of our help. Judging someone is tantamount to kicking them when they are down.

If we are willing to embrace our destiny, we give up using others and problems to hold us back. We recognise others' genuine calls for help in their missteps and mistakes. We are willing to give up hiding and be who we truly are in all of our genius, magnificence and mastery.

Exercise

Today, for your own sake and the world, examine your life for how you may be avoiding yourself and who you have come to be. Reflect on how you may be hiding and how your life is your conspiracy against yourself. Take a close look at how you may be using the person with whom you are not getting along to avoid what's really important in your life, such as your destiny.

Is it worth it to try to run from yourself and your destiny throughout your whole life in an attempt to be safe? You may achieve some degree of anonymity and relative safety, but you can never be true to yourself or others and you will forsake happiness, missing the opportunity to do what you can to help. And you will not keep your promise to God, yourself or humanity.

Examine what precious and unique gifts you have brought to help humanity. Today you can decide to be willing to give your gifts in this life. In truth, all that is required is your willingness to give up being the rebel. Choose today to give your gifts, as every problem with another person is just a place where we are not rediscovering and giving a gift within us.

Glossary

Bonding The connection that exists between us and others. Bonding creates love and success with ease rather than with struggle and difficulty. It is what gives cohesiveness its glue and teamwork its mutuality.

Compensation This is what psychologists call 'reaction formation'. It is a role that is meant to hide and make up for negative feelings, and it is meant to prove that we are positive, innocent and desiring of love. When there is compensation present, we act in an opposite way, as a reaction to a mistaken feeling. However, it doesn't allow us to receive because it is not true giving. It is a mechanism of proving. Unfortunately, much of what we do can be considered compensation. But it's a wasted effort and an attempt to prove what doesn't need proving – namely our innocence and value.

Conspiracy A chronic trap of the ego, set up so well that it looks like we will never escape it. Conspiracies are particularly difficult to heal until we realise that the problem has been set up that way.

Ego The part of us that seeks separation and specialness and – ultimately – wants to be God. It is the part of us that fights for itself and its own needs first. It is built on fear, guilt, negativity, and competition, wanting to be the best of something, even if it is painful, or the best of the worst. Ego distracts, delays and attempts to stop evolution, being more concerned with its own continuity. It is based on domination-subjugation, rather than any form of strength or truth. It is ultimately an illusion. We make it strong, while we are young, and then melt it away for partnership and grace.

Fusion A muddling of boundaries that occurs when bonding is lost. We cannot tell where we end and another begins. Fusion is the ego's answer to the lost intimacy. It is counterfeit bonding, which creates sacrifice and builds resentment. Fusion sets up an overburdening sense of loyalty. This eventually causes us to burn out and move into the opposite extreme of independence. We move from over-caring and smothering to acting as if we do not care.

Gifts Aspects of greatness or grace that make any job easy. Our gifts are the answer to all situations because they remove the problem. Gifts are learned lessons that continuously give and create flow. They are packets of wisdom, healing and responsiveness for the situation at hand. In every problem, there is a potential gift. We have thousands of unopened gifts within us that are the antidote to pain and problems.

Higher Mind The aspect of the mind that is creative, contains or receives all of our answers, opens our will and our spirit to the grace that heaven and the world around us wants to bestow on us. It is always guiding us with a quiet voice toward the truth. It encourages us to win together, not only now, but in the future.

Love This is the ultimate goal and the best means to the goal. It is the sweet fulfilment that comes of an open-hearted extension of oneself. This is the giving, receiving, sharing and reaching out to one another. Love is the foundation of being and the best description of God, whatever your religious beliefs. It gives us everything we want – meaning, happiness, healing, nurturing and joy. Our evolution and happiness are based on how much we give and receive in love.

Manifest Consciously using the mind to choose what we want. It is the use of visualisation, feeling and sensing what we want, and then letting it go and trusting. It allows us to create exactly what we want in detail.

Sacrifice A psychological mistake in which we give and don't receive. It's a role that compensates for feelings of failure, guilt and unworthiness. It hides competition and taking, and it attempts to lose now to win later. A script of sacrifice tells a story of us losing for others to win at a time when a script could be written for everyone to win. Sacrifice is afraid of the intimacy that brings equality.

Scarcity A fear-based belief that there is not enough and that we, or someone else, will have to go without. A belief in scarcity sets up power struggle, competition and sacrifice.

Shadow Figures Self-concepts that we have judged about ourselves and as a result, repressed. They represent areas of self-hatred that we project out onto others around us or onto the world in general.

Tantrum A choice in which we react, complain, withdraw or hurt ourselves when life does not come about as we consciously want. It can show itself as any form of failure, immaturity, or lack of success.

The stages of relationships

All relationships go through stages on their way to making heaven on earth. Each stage has its own challenges, traps and answers. If you know the stages of relationship, you are better prepared to handle the challenges and not to be blind-sided by the issues.

1. Relationships begin in the Romance or Honeymoon Stage, where we idealise the other, yet it is in this stage that we can see and feel the potential of the relationship.
2. Then there is the Power Struggle Stage where we are learning to bridge our differences, communicate, join and integrate both positions. Here we project out our shadow figures on our partner, and primarily fight for our needs.
3. The Dead Zone is a stage where we are learning to transcend good form for authenticity, find our worth without roles or sacrifice and learn how to bond, moving beyond the counterfeit bonding of fusion.
4. The Partnership Stage is where we have

reached a balance between our own masculine-feminine sides and, correspondingly, we do so in our relationship with our partner, finding balance, equality and intimacy.

5. The Leadership Stage is where we have both become leaders in life and have learned to value each other beyond the conflict and competition of personalities.

6. The Vision Stage occurs when we have become a visionary along with our partner, making contributions to the earth and healing unconscious pain and fractures.

7. The Mastery Stage of relationships is where we have healed our feelings of failure and valuelessness to the point of moving from doing and becoming, to being and grace. This is where we become living treasures to the earth. It is the beginning of heaven on earth for our relationship.

Further Information

About the Psychology of Vision

PSYCHOLOGY
VISION of.

For details on other books, the full range of audio
and videotapes, and world-wide seminars, please
contact us at:
   Psychology of Vision UK
   France Farm
   Rushall
   Pewsey
   Wiltshire SN9 6DR
   UK
   Tel: +44 (0)1980 635199
   e-mail: promotions@psychologyofvision.com
   website: www.psychologyofvision.com

Also by Chuck Spezzano
(and available from the Psychology of Vision):
The Enlightenment Pack
Awaken the Gods